TRUE
STORIES
OF
ANSWERED
PRAYER

TRUE STORIES *of* ANSWERED PRAYER

MIKE NAPPA

TYNDALE HOUSE PUBLISHERS, INC.
WHEATON, ILLINOIS

Visit Tyndale's exciting Web site at www.tyndale.com

True Stories of Answered Prayer is another creative resource from the authors at Nappaland Communications, Inc. To contact the author, send email to Nappaland@aol.com

Designed by Jackie Noe

Edited by Chimena Kabasenche

The story "My Only Prayer" by Lee Maynard, which appears on page 173 of this book, is reprinted by permission from the author. Copyright © 1997 by Lee Maynard. Originally published in the April 1998 issue of *Reader's Digest*.

Unless otherwise indicated, all Scripture quotations are taken from the *Holy Bible,* New Living Translation, copyright © 1996. Used by permission of Tyndale House Publishers, Inc., Wheaton, Illinois 60189. All rights reserved.

Library of Congress Cataloging-in-Publication Data

Nappa, Mike, date
  True stories of answered prayer / Mike Nappa.
    p. cm.
  ISBN 0-8423-5178-7 (hc : alk. paper)
  1. Prayer—Christianity. I. Title.
BV220.N36 1999
242—dc21   99-22980

Printed in the United States of America

05 04 03 02 01 00 99
10 9 8 7 6 5 4 3 2 1

For Amy, my partner in prayer and in life.
You, my dear, are my answer to prayer.
I love you!
M. N.

"The beauty of prayer is that anyone can pray.
You don't have to be a certain age,
you don't have to have wealth,
you don't have to have a certain talent
— all you have to have is a stubborn faith
and a willingness to intercede."

MAX LUCADO, *Walking with the Savior*

Contents

Acknowledgments

I would like to gratefully acknowledge a few important people. First, Meg Diehl, Tyndale's former acquisitions editor, whose passion for this book overcame my initial decision not to write it.

Next, Lee Maynard, who graciously allowed me to reprint his touching story of answered prayer word for word in this book. Thank you, Lee, for your kindness to me, a stranger.

Also, I can't write a book on prayer without acknowledging the one woman who showed me the power of prayer through her own life: my mother, Dr. Zahea Nappa. It is she who has prayed for me since before I was born. It was her prayers that helped me through a less-than-perfect childhood and turbulent teen years and her prayers that continue to strengthen my family and me today. I am grateful beyond words for the power of her prayers in my life.

Last, but certainly not least, I wish to acknowledge Jesus Christ, my Lord, my Savior, my highest reason for living. If I had not met him nearly two decades ago, I truly would have nothing to write about. Ever. The words of the old hymn proclaim:

What a privilege to carry everything to God in prayer!

Introduction

"There is hardly any human activity—including getting up in the morning, exercising, working, driving, eating, having sex, watching TV, reading, talking to people, and going to bed at night—that someone doesn't associate with prayer," says religious researcher Jim Castelli.[1]

Take one look at your life, and you know he's right. Take a look at American life in general, and you see it even more clearly. Consider:

• Nine out of ten Americans say they pray. Seventy-five percent of Americans report praying *every day*.[2]

• *Life* magazine reported that 98 percent of Americans pray for their families, 92 percent pray for forgiveness. And one of every four Americans even prays for seemingly inconsequential things like victory in a sports event.[3]

• When we pray, nearly half of us do it for about five minutes or less, but 28 percent of us put in an hour or more.[4]

• The results of all this prayer? More than 200 million Americans (95 percent) report having experienced answers to prayer.[5]

In spite of this, our prevailing attitude toward prayer is summed up in words like the

1. Jim Castelli, "Prayer," USA Weekend, 23–25 December 1994.
2. Ibid.
3. "Why We Pray," Life (March 1994): 58.
4. Ibid, 60.
5. Ibid, 62.

ones these teenagers wrote on the message boards on America Online:[6]

"I believe in God, but I don't think God answers every prayer. One in ten thousand maybe."

"Any thoughts on prayer? Yeah. It's dumb."

"I'm curious what makes people [pray]. It seems pointless to me."

This book is for those teenagers—and for everyone else who has ever felt abandoned by God, unsure of prayer, and ready to give up hope. When you feel discouraged, let the stories in this book remind you not only that there is a God but also that he is constantly at work in the lives of people like you and me—even when we can't see it, don't feel it, and won't believe it.

All the events recorded in this book are true instances I've collected through interviews, casual conversations, email queries, written surveys, and personal experience. In some cases names have been changed or deliberately omitted to protect the privacy of the individuals involved.

But there's one name that is always the same: the name of Jesus Christ, the one to whom each prayer recorded in this book was first directed. Now, as you begin reading about the answered prayers of others, may Jesus meet you within each page and remind you that God never abandons those who seek him (see Psalm 9:10).
Mike Nappa, 1998

6. Mike Nappa, "When God Seems Silent," Group's Real Life Bible Curriculum (1995): 6.

A PRAYER
FOR THE SHEPHERD

Andrae Crouch needed his sleep. It takes a lot of
time and energy to be a gospel music singer, pastor
of a church, and leader of a street outreach
program in urban Los Angeles. And with the
recent discovery of three cancerous tumors in his
body, Pastor Crouch needed to do all he could do
to keep his body healthy.

He was so weary he was tempted not to answer
the phone when it woke him up at three-thirty
in the morning. He was sleeping in the office/
apartment attached to Christ Memorial Church,
where he pastored, and he wanted to go back to
sleep. Still, the call had come in on his private,
unlisted line, so he reluctantly reached for the
receiver.

"Hello?" he said.

A woman's voice, heavy with a Spanish accent,
responded, "Is this the Memorial Church?"

"Yes."

The voice on the phone was firm. "I am to pray for the shepherd."

Andrae was wide awake now. As pastor of Christ Memorial, he was often called the shepherd of his church.

Without hesitation, the woman began to pray, "Father, in the name of Jesus, I pray for the infirmity of this shepherd, and I curse it. I curse it at the root, and it is gone in the name of Jesus."

Then she hung up.

Pastor Crouch lay awake a few moments, wondering how the woman had gotten his phone number, how she knew he had an infirmity, and why she'd called to pray in the wee hours of the morning. He finally returned to sleep.

2

Two days later Andrae reported to the doctor's office for a checkup. The doctor wanted to assess how quickly the cancer was growing and to begin making recommendations for treatment.

After searching for the tumors for about ten minutes, the doctor put a hand on his hip. "Maybe you can find them, Pastor Crouch, because I don't feel anything."

Andrae pointed and said, "Well, they're here, remember? The big one's right . . . right . . ." Suddenly his eyes filled with tears.

All three of the tumors were gone.

2

WALKING
DISTANCE

"Dear Jesus . . ." Four-year-old Tony started his
bedtime prayer in the same fashion he always did,
continuing through the customary list of relatives and
his dog (named after a Disney character). "Help my
mom, my dad, me and Aladdin, Jody and Erik, Jill
and Annette, Grandma and Grandpa all to sleep well."

But this night, instead of ending the prayer as
he normally would, Tony added an extra line:
"Please help Aunt Jody and Uncle Erik move to a
house within walking distance of ours. Amen."

The trouble was that Tony lived in Colorado,
while Jody and Erik lived in southern California.
Jody had been working as a freelance writer for a
publishing company in Colorado, and it was
possible the company might need a new editor in
the coming months.

Tony continued to pray. Each night before bed,

he diligently asked Jesus to arrange for Jody and Erik to move "within walking distance" of his home.

Over the course of the next few months, that editorial job did open up. After a lengthy interview process, Jody was chosen to fill the position. Erik and Jody were moving to Tony's town!

But where would they live? Tony never wavered. He kept on praying his special prayer. When Erik got a job in a nearby city and considered moving a twenty-minute car drive to the north, Tony prayed. When Erik and Jody decided to move to an outlying area about fifteen minutes to the west, Tony prayed. When they found a rental a block away, Tony thought his prayer had been answered—but the house was rented to someone else.

Shortly thereafter, the house next to the rental went up for sale. It was well kept, just the right size, close to a small park in a quiet neighborhood, near Jody's work, and within driving distance of Erik's. Best of all, it was within walking distance of Tony's house. Everyone was thrilled . . . until they found out the house had been sold the day before Jody and Erik made an offer. It seemed like Tony would have to settle for having his favorite aunt and uncle live within driving distance.

Then one day Jody and Erik got a call. The original buyer of the house by the park had backed out, and the homeowner had kept Jody and Erik's number "just in case." The owner wanted to know if the couple still liked the house.

A few weeks later Tony himself was in charge of carrying the couch cushions when Jody and Erik moved into that special house—"within walking distance."

HIGH AND DRY
IN BUDAPEST

In 1988 Eastern Europe was ruled by the
Communist Soviet Union. John and Katherine
Wilhelm felt sure God was leading them behind
the Iron Curtain to share with others the news
of Jesus Christ and his resurrection.

After months of study and outreach in the
Soviet Union, John and Katherine were traveling
by train to Budapest, Hungary. There, they were
to meet a missionary, who would care for them
and see them on the way to their next destination
of Vienna, Austria.

The train lurched into the station at 7:00 A.M.,
Budapest time. After thirty-three hours of travel,
John and Katherine were looking forward to resting
and bathing at the home of the missionaries
scheduled to meet them. They gathered their
luggage and made their way to the crowded

platform. They spotted a bench, sat down, and waited for their Hungarian contacts to pick them up.

After an hour, no one had come. John tried to call the missionaries. No answer. He tried to call the office in Germany that had coordinated their trip. Again, no answer. John went back to the bench and waited with Katherine.

They waited a long time.

Five hours later they were still stranded on the bench in a crowded train station, thousands of miles from home, unable to speak the language, and thereby unable to communicate their need to anyone but God. They whispered several prayers to the one who understands all languages and asked for help and guidance out of Budapest.

John and Katherine tried calling the office in Germany again. Finally, Katherine was able to get through. She was told there had been a mix-up. The missionaries who were to meet them had traveled to America for a brief furlough. John and Katherine would have to make their way to Vienna on their own.

Near tears, Katherine hung up the phone and walked back to where John was waiting. Overcome with hopelessness, she sighed aloud, "Lord, what are we going to do?"

Suddenly, an elderly man in front of her turned and said clearly, "You speak English."

Katherine was stunned, then overjoyed. "*You* speak English!"

"Yes, I used to live here in Hungary, but many years ago I moved to New Zealand. I'm here visiting friends." He paused. "Now, what is your trouble?"

Although it was a risk to tell a stranger her missionary goals in a Communist country, Katherine said a quick prayer and then explained her predicament.

The man nodded. "I will help you."

For the next hour he helped John and Katherine make the necessary arrangements. First, they needed a place to stay. After checking around, they found that the cheapest available hotel room cost $100—more than they had. A few moments later they were standing in line at the post office, and the man struck up a conversation with the woman behind him. All but the man seemed surprised to find out she had a spare bedroom she was willing to let them use for the night for only a ten-dollar fee—she agreed to transport them from the train station and back and to make dinner and breakfast for them as well!

Next, the man brought Katherine to the currency-exchange building. Ignoring hour-long lines, the man strode up to the counter without protest from anyone. He helped Katherine exchange her money so she could buy train tickets for the trip to Vienna the next morning.

When all the details were covered and the man was certain John and Katherine had been taken care of, he shook John's hand and looked him straight in the eye. "God bless you."

John was so surprised to hear him speak of God in public, he turned to tell Katherine. When he turned back a half second later, the man was gone.

4

THE ANSWER'S
IN THE CAN

What do you do when you're the oldest of four
children, when there's barely any food in your
family's cupboard, and when your church is having
a canned-food drive to help needy families on
Thanksgiving?

Thirteen-year-old Anne wasn't sure, but she
knew she had to do something.

According to her Sunday school teacher, each
child was to bring one nonperishable item to the
morning church service that week. Those items
would be gathered into baskets and given that
evening to poorer families in the community
for Thanksgiving dinner. Anne looked in the
cupboard and found two cans of vegetables, a box
of macaroni, and a bag of rice—four nonperishable
items, one for each child in her family.

But giving those items to the canned-food drive
left nothing for Anne's family. After pausing for a

brief prayer, Anne felt that God was directing her to help those needy families by giving the food. With a deep sigh, she gathered the items in the cupboard and distributed them to her siblings. When they put the nonperishable goods in the collection at church, Anne prayed again that God would use their gifts and provide for her family as well.

After church Anne and her family played away the Sunday with games, television, football, and books. That afternoon the doorbell rang. Standing at the door were representatives from her church; in their arms they held baskets overflowing with food for the holiday.

Anne's family had been chosen to receive the gifts her church had donated to the canned-food drive—including the four items her family had given. That Thanksgiving their cupboard was full.

5

CAMERON
DANTE

"Cameron Dante was a pop star in England," says Andy Hawthorne, leader of the popular Christian dance band from Britain called The World Wide Message Tribe.

"He had four top ten hits," Andy continues, "[and] he's an amazing dancer. He was the U.K. break-dancing champion and third in the world championships and . . . an amazing rapper—just a great communicator. Trouble was, he was off his face on drugs most of the time."

When Cameron decided to record an album at the studio used by The World Wide Message Tribe, Andy and his bandmates decided it was time to pray. For the next six months the band prayed for Cameron each day.

They prayed that God would change his heart and lead him out of the jungle of drugs and clubs and parties that went along with the lifestyle of a pop superstar. They prayed Cameron would one day meet and be changed by Jesus Christ.

While Cameron was recording his album, The World Wide Message Tribe's producer had an opportunity to tell Cameron about what faith in Christ meant. Cameron hesitated to make a decision at that point, but he agreed to come to a church service where the band was scheduled to play.

Andy chuckles. "He came to one [church service]. The first one he came to, he gave his life to Christ."

Cameron was transformed almost immediately; he burned with zeal for God and the Bible. Then he did what seemed to be the natural thing to do. He went home and told his live-in girlfriend all about it. She became angry. Like Cameron, she loved the party scene, even performing regularly as a cage dancer in a nightclub. She didn't like that Cameron had gotten so caught up in religion, but she couldn't help noticing a difference in him. It wasn't long before she wanted that difference too. Cameron's girlfriend became a Christian.

Nine months after his conversion, Cameron Dante left his mainstream music career and joined The World Wide Message Tribe as a vocalist. Eighteen months after he became a Christian, Cameron and his girlfriend married. Andy Hawthorne preached at the wedding, and the band performed at the reception.

"It's probably the most exciting thing I've ever seen, those two," says Andy. "Praying for somebody who's about as far away from God as you can imagine. And then to see that process of God working in their life, them being set on fire [with a] hunger for the Bible and prayer and then see *them* start winning people. It's fantastic."

6

A CHRISTMAS WISH

The sleepy town of Odyssey is a magical place.
Children in this fictional city are constantly treated
to a world of wonder, excitement, and adventure!
There's Whit's End, a soda shop and discovery
emporium that's often the center of action in the
town. There's buried treasure, a spy ring, churches,
politicians, greedy merchants, and unsuspecting
children. But no matter what's going on, Jesus is
the hero constantly working in the lives of his
children.

When Phil Lollar cocreated this wonderful
world more than a decade ago for Focus on the
Family, he could not have imagined that the
Adventures in Odyssey radio program would grow
to become a family tradition. In addition to novels
and animated videos, *Adventures in Odyssey* has
been translated into fifteen languages and has aired
on radio.

But thirty-four years earlier, on Christmas Eve in 1964, the writer/producer/actor who launched Odyssey was just a five-year-old child who missed his daddy.

Little Phil and his family were living in Klamath Falls, Oregon, at the time, staying with the boy's grandparents. For many years Phil's father had suffered from asthma, and 1964 was especially bad. His father had to go south to a hospital in San Francisco for treatment. For the first time in Phil's life, Christmas would come and go without his father being there.

The family celebrated the holiday as best they could. They sang carols, ate Christmas dinner, played, and happily anticipated opening their presents. Still, for one young kindergartner, it just wasn't the same. How could it be Christmas while Daddy lay wheezing in a hospital bed many miles away?

In a bit of holiday kindness, Phil's mother allowed him and his older brother to sleep under the dining-room table on Christmas Eve. When they awoke, it would be Christmas; they would be close to the tree.

Phil got comfortable under the table and waited for sleep to come. As he closed his eyes, he prayed to himself, *Lord, all I want for Christmas is my Daddy*. Heavyhearted in spite of the holiday, he drifted off to sleep.

The night was still black when Phil felt his mother gently shaking him awake. Was it Christmas Day already? No, it was only midnight. Why was his mother insisting he wake up?

Sleepily rubbing his eyes, Phil followed Mom to his parents' bedroom. There, sitting up in bed, was Daddy. The hospital had released him so he could come home in time to spend Christmas Day with his family. Phil felt an inexpressible joy. Daddy was home!

Phil still thinks fondly of that 1964 Christmas. "I knew from that moment on—no doubt in my mind—that God answers prayer."

7

MISERY LOVES
COMPANY

Andy Chrisman was miserable. There's no other
way to describe it. He was out-and-out miserable.

The year was 1987, and Andy was sitting in his
apartment feeling certain that the whole world
wanted him unhappy. He was attending college,
trying to make his way through the career maze
that confronted him, but he wasn't enjoying it.
His grades were good, but he felt discontented,
discouraged, and disillusioned. His whole life at
that point seemed meaningless, just a daily
collection of useless activities.

In short, he was a miserable wreck.

Since misery loves company, Andy didn't bear
his sorrow alone. He cried out to God, begging
the Lord to reveal his will to him. Should he stay
in college, work toward a degree, prepare for a
career, and save money for his future? Should he
skip out of college and pursue his dream of being a

Christian singer? Should he ignore those ideas and be a janitor, fulfilling God's will by serving others in an often-unappreciated position?

Andy didn't know what to do, but he knew he wanted God to be involved—no matter what. He sat in his room, praying, imploring his Creator, "God, use me. Whatever you want me to do, I'll do. Just use me!" After Andy's prayer time was over, nothing had really changed. At least he had been able to share his misery with One who cared and who could help.

The next day Andy waited for a word from God to let him know that God had heard his prayer. Nothing happened. The second day came and went without a whisper.

The third day Andy's phone rang. On the other end was the leader of the Christian music ensemble Truth. "Andy, there's an opening in Truth, and we want you to come audition for the group. If you pass the audition, we'd like you to join us for our road tour. Will you come try out?"

Andy enthusiastically agreed. He joined Truth and toured with them. A few years later, in 1989, he and three other guys started the vocal group 4Him. The band members have performed worldwide in their ministry. 4Him has recorded more than six albums. Ten of their songs have been number-one hit songs on Christian radio; they have won three Dove Awards. The group members of 4Him speak unapologetically about faith and experience.

"Just use me," Andy Chrisman prayed in 1987. God answered that prayer with a phone call, using

that little spark to launch a music ministry. Andy
says with confidence, "I believe so much in prayer.
I believe in specific prayer. . . . My wife and I
practice it as much as we can!"

8

HOLE
IN THE SKY

Don Weber loved to fly. Nothing else in the world could bring the peace and beauty of winging through the clouds, of literally touching the sky. Don enjoyed many opportunities to fly because of his job as a missionary aviator to the jungle tribes of the Amazon basin.

Don regularly flew his single-engine plane across the Amazonian expanse, noting landmarks and rivers that would guide him safely through the uncharted jungle. He didn't fly those routes alone. Don was the pilot, but he trusted God to be the navigator leading him safely to his destination and back home to his family.

One gray day, Don walked up the runway to his plane and surveyed the sky. The clouds were turning black; the wind whipped at his clothes. If he flew now, he might make it home to his wife and children ahead of the oncoming storm.

Strapping himself into the cockpit, Don revved the engine, taxied down the airstrip, and zoomed into space. Keeping an eye on the snaking brown river below, Don carefully pointed his plane in the right direction and settled in for the journey home.

The flight went well at first—a little bumpy but navigable. Then, with frightening speed, the threatening rain exploded into a full-scale jungle monsoon. Don's plane bounced and groaned, straining against the wind and rain that buffeted everything in sight. Menacing clouds billowed and rolled, surrounding the missionary and blocking his view of the ground below.

With visibility gone, Don knew he had to get to safety immediately, or he would never make it home. His only hope was to return to the airstrip he'd just left. Banking his plane through the monsoon, Don turned to go back—and was greeted by massive, impenetrable cloud cover. There was no way out. Effectively blinded by the storm, he braced for the worst and prayed.

"This is it, Lord! My life is in your hands!" Don readied himself for the crash landing that would probably kill him.

He gazed through the cockpit window, awaiting death. Then, slowly but unmistakably, he noticed a change in the storm. Like heavy blankets being tossed aside, the clouds ahead began piling up and shifting. Directly in front of him, as if in response to an unheard command, the billows rolled away; a bright hole appeared in the sky—a path of visibility through the storm.

Watching the miracle unfold around him, Don

shot forward into the opening, thinking that this must have been how the Israelites felt when God parted the Red Sea to allow them to pass. The path in the air stayed open, a quiet spot surrounded by the storm. Before long Don spotted the airstrip and made his way to a safe landing.

As the plane's wheels whined to a stop on the runway, Don heaved a sigh of relief and turned to view his miracle once more. He saw the opening suddenly collapse, overtaken by the torrential rain and wind.

God, the Great Navigator, had made a way where there was no way. Don was safely on the ground. God had answered Don's prayer, leaving the aviator to worship and wonder at the power of his mighty Savior.

25

9

ON A MISSION
OF PRAYER

Denise Hildreth had her own problems. She was
sitting in the hospital lobby crying because one of
her family members was near death. All Denise
could do was sit, wait, cry, and pray.

Looking around the lobby, Denise noticed
another family. Like her, they were expressing
sorrow. Denise wondered what had caused· their
tears. As she got up to leave the lobby area, she felt
compelled to stop before the exit. Hesitating for a
moment, she thought to herself, *I'm going to see
what they need. Maybe I can offer a prayer or something.*

Denise walked over to the sorrowful family and
inquired about their situation. The mother had
heart failure, and she was in that hospital hovering
between life and death. The family had lost hope.
They were beside themselves trying to prepare for
the great loss of this loved one.

Denise quickly realized there was little she could

do to change the situation, but she determined to do *something*. "I do believe in prayer, and I do believe in Christ. All I can do is pray for you."

The family members all bowed their heads while Denise prayed a simple prayer, asking Jesus to heal and restore to this family the mother they were afraid of losing. Then Denise walked out of the room and, she thought, out of that family's life.

Later that week Denise was at the hospital to visit her family member, who was recovering quickly. As she made her way down the hall, she spied a group of people who looked familiar. Yes, it was the family she had stopped to pray with a few days earlier!

Something was different this time. Instead of frowning, they were smiling. Instead of crying, they were laughing. Instead of grieving, they were chatting freely.

When that family saw Denise, they stopped to fill her in. After Denise's prayer, their mother had unexpectedly begun improving. In fact, she was doing so well, the doctors thought she could return home in the next few days! God was answering Denise's prayer, working a miraculous healing inside the mother's heart.

Denise smiled. Yes, she still had problems, but pausing to pray for that family *had* made a difference. The news lightened Denise's own burdens.

Denise told her husband about the outcome of her prayer, and the two of them sat down to write a song about the experience. The name of the song is "To Be a Christian." You can hear Denise's husband, Jonathan Pierce, sing about it on his 1997 album, *Mission*.

10

ADDITION
AND SUBTRACTION

The numbers just didn't add up. Craig Keener
sighed and pushed aside the page that held his
budget for the next year. No matter what he did,
Craig couldn't figure out a way for his income to
match the expected expenses. Fresh out of school,
unemployed, and needing a large amount of
money soon, he wasn't sure what to do next.

Craig was not a man without resources. He had
sketched a scholarly study of the New Testament,
resulting in some eighty thousand note cards
detailing the historical context of nearly every
passage of Scripture from Matthew to Revelation.

Craig had hoped that a Christian publisher
would be interested in having him write a
contemporary commentary on the New
Testament. Unfortunately, his efforts remained
fruitless. Even if someone wanted to buy his
commentary, there was little hope they would pay

him enough to live on during the year he would write it!

Craig had recently completed a seminary degree. Surely that was worth something—but what? Perhaps he could find a pastoral job somewhere. Maybe he could be a teacher at a Bible school.

Craig sighed again. His eyes kept coming back to that figure at the bottom of the page, the amount of money he'd need to make it through the next year. It seemed impossible. But he knew Someone who specialized in doing the impossible: God.

Before Craig Keener went to bed that night in 1990, he spent some time in prayer with God. Talking about the subject of his budget, Craig pointed out that he didn't know how or where to earn the money he needed to cover his upcoming expenses. He pleaded with God to help him find a way. He did his best to turn the whole matter over to God and went to bed trusting that somehow, someway, God would provide.

The next morning came as normal. The sun rose. The alarm went off. Craig greeted the day and waited for a miracle. This day, the miracle would come in the form of a phone call.

On the other end of the line was an editor at the Christian publishing house InterVarsity Press. Craig could hardly believe his ears. They wanted him to write a commentary! He felt like holding his breath as they outlined the terms. They came to the part about the royalty advance they'd pay Craig while he worked on the book.

The editor named a figure.

Craig felt like shouting. The figure the editor named was *exactly* the same number he had written on his budget and had prayed about the night before. God had answered his prayer in dramatic fashion.

Dr. Craig S. Keener wrote his book, published in 1993 as *The IVP Bible Background Commentary: New Testament.* Going verse by verse through the New Testament, Craig shared his knowledge on the historical background surrounding the Bible. Thus, he created an invaluable resource for Christians who wish to understand a bit more of what they read in the Scriptures.

11

LITTLE
RED GEO

"My fellow bandmates and friends tell me that my life is just a long list of miracles," laughs Erik Sundin, lead singer for the Christian reggae band Temple Yard. "God just provides and provides and provides. It's just amazing."

Before starting Temple Yard in 1998, Erik was the lead singer of the pioneer Christian reggae group Christafari. Until Christafari, most people assumed that the Jamaican drug culture and Rastafari religion associated with reggae preempted Christian music of the same style. Christafari not only made it possible but also excelled at it. Call that miracle number one.

Miracle number two was the group's immediate acceptance both in Christian circles and in reggae circles. The band played all the major Christian festivals and toured with the high-profile main-stream event Reggae Sunsplash. They charted top

33

ten hits in *Billboard Magazine,* performed at the 1996 Summer Olympics, and played at the 1997 Presidential Inaugural Ball in Washington, D.C.

But for Erik Sundin those miracles pale in comparison to the personal miracles he's experienced. Despite the success of Christafari, Erik had to work part-time as a delivery driver in Nashville, Tennessee, in 1996. One night, Erik loaded his car with sumptuous goodies and headed for the address on his delivery slip. Rain poured from the sky, filling the streets of Music City with little rivers running through traffic. Turning a corner, Erik unexpectedly hit a current in the pavement, and his car started to hydroplane.

He had a sickening feeling when his car began "surfing." He steered and nothing happened. He pounded on the breaks, yet his car didn't slow. All Erik could do was watch helplessly as his vehicle, skidding at about thirty miles per hour, careened into a brick wall.

The auto was completely totaled, with all four wheels bent under the chassis and the engine crushed. Thankfully, Eric walked away from the accident unharmed. Call that miracle number three.

Not only was Erik's car lost, but the wreck had jeopardized his job. After all, how can a guy make deliveries without a car? Erik prayed for another miracle. He and his wife prayed together, asking God to provide a new means of transportation in spite of their low funds. Erik recruited friends to pray for him, including Matt O'Conner, a staff member at Erik's church.

Family and friends prayed for three days, and on the third day Erik got a phone call while away from his home. It was Matt. "God has answered your prayers, man. I'll see you when you get to your house."

When Erik arrived, he found a red 1990 Geo Storm parked in the driveway. With a smile on his face, Matt announced to Erik, "This is yours."

An anonymous person in the church felt God leading him to give away this car, but he didn't know anybody who needed one. The man approached Matt O'Conner to see if he knew anyone in need of reliable transportation—and Matt immediately told him about Erik. When the car was delivered to Erik's door, prayers of all three men were miraculously answered.

Erik Sundin remains grateful for the way God responded to his prayer by providing a little red Geo Storm. "I still have it," he reports with pride. "Still running!"

12

THROUGH
THE UPRIGHTS

Coming out of college in 1993, kicker Todd
Peterson was thrilled to be drafted in the seventh
round by the New York Giants—most kickers
aren't drafted at all!

Todd couldn't wait to fulfill his dream of being
a professional football player. Then, before the
season began, the thrill turned to disappointment.
The Giants cut Todd from their roster, opting to
go with veteran David Treadwell instead.

Todd still had opportunities to try out with
other NFL teams: Washington, Miami, New
England, Arizona, Pittsburgh, Cincinnati. One by
one, those teams all said the same thing: "Thanks,
but no thanks." Todd earned tryouts with over a
dozen teams. Nobody took him.

"Basically, all those teams were saying, 'We're
not willing to take a chance on you right now.
You need to get into a game.' And I kept thinking

to myself, *How do you get into a game unless somebody takes a chance on you?"*

Frustrated, Todd went to the place he knew he'd always be accepted—straight to Jesus. "Finally, I just got on my knees one day and was like, 'God, what's going on here? If you want me to play pro football, then *you've* got to open the doors. If you don't want me to play, then take the desire out of my heart.' "

Todd didn't hear anything from God right away, but he did start getting encouragement from teams. "Teams continued to tell me, 'You're going to be good. You're going to be good.' So I finally said, 'Lord, I'm going to trust that the sign you're giving me is that you want me to keep plugging away at this. . . . I'm going to trust that you want me doing it.' And that's what my approach was."

In May 1994 that faith and perseverance seemed to pay off. The Atlanta Falcons signed this up-and-coming field-goal specialist to their team! . . . And cut him just days before the opening game. Todd could hardly bear his disappointment. The 1994 season started, but Todd was still grounded in the bleachers, watching the action from afar. Then, unexpectedly, he got another chance to prove what he could do in the NFL.

In October of that year, Arizona Cardinals kicker Greg Davis went down with an injury. Arizona needed someone to fill Davis's spot for a few weeks. Remembering his solid tryout months before, the Cardinals turned to Todd.

On October 16, 1994, Todd played in his first NFL game against the Washington Redskins, a team that had passed him up earlier. Todd went out ready to make the 'Skins sorry they'd let him go . . . and promptly missed a field goal that could have given the Cardinals enough points to win the game.

Still, at the end of regulation, the score was tied at sixteen. With 4:56 minutes left in the overtime period, the Cardinals coach called on Todd once more, now asking him to win the game.

Todd said a quick prayer and tried not to let the pressure get to him. *Kick the game-winning field goal and be a hero, or miss it and walk out of the NFL forever.* The ball was hiked and set. Todd went through his routine. . . . And this time he booted the football through the uprights for the win. On the strength of his performance as a substitute kicker for the Cardinals, the Seattle Seahawks signed Todd Peterson to a multiyear contract starting with the 1995 season. He was a full-time pro at last.

With the Seahawks, Todd set several team records, including most points scored in a season. He was chosen as the AFC Special Teams Player of the Week. Through all the honors, the wins and losses, and the pressures and temptations of life in the NFL, Todd remains focused on what really matters: his relationship with Jesus.

"God has been gracious to me. God gave me the talent, and he's blessed me. He's been gracious to allow me to use that talent to glorify him." He shakes his head in wonder. "That has been an amazing thing for me."

13

NINE HUNDRED
THOUSAND SHILLINGS

Nine hundred thousand shillings is how much
home currency Tony Ombogo of Kenya, Africa,
needed to pay for his first year of school at a
Christian college in the United States. Because
of his status as an international student, he had to
have all that money in hand before the U.S. would
issue his visa.

Assuming Tony worked seven days a week and
saved every bit from his twenty-seven-shilling-a-
day job as a telephone technician, Tony figured it
would be ninety-one years before he could start his
freshman year.

To compound the problem, financial aid
monies were unavailable for Tony. He explains,
"As an international student, I cannot receive any
assistance for my first year. I do not even receive
federal aid when I'm in school."

Tony prayed for God's help, asking him to

somehow provide the money he needed to pursue his dream of becoming a medical missionary. Despite fervent prayer, Tony was ready to give up. It looked like his dream would die.

Looking back on that time in his life, Tony reflects, "I didn't think it would happen."

But God had a different idea, and it came in the form of Tony's dad.

Tony's father was determined to make it possible for Tony to pursue his dream at Emmanuel College in Franklin Springs, Georgia. "My first year, I think my dad made that happen," Tony says proudly. His dad talked to friends, colleagues, and anyone else who would listen. He called about 150 relatives and family friends, inviting them to come to a special reunion/fund-raiser for Tony.

On the appointed day, around seventy people showed up. Tony reports, "Everybody [brought] as much as they could and dropped it in a bucket. At the end of the day, we collected about five hundred thousand Kenya shillings."

Slowly but surely, the Ombogo family saw money trickling in. On the day the fall semester began at Emmanuel, Tony had the tuition money! He had scraped together funds to cover room and board, and he even held his travel visa in hand. . . .

But he was 144,000 shillings short of the amount needed to purchase a plane ticket to America. While he languished at home in Africa, classes started without him.

God then revealed that he has a sense of humor. Tony was traveling to a *Christian* college, but a

Hindu businessman responded to a request by Tony's father and agreed to provide the needed plane ticket.

Tony arrived at Emmanuel College two weeks into the semester, quickly enrolled in classes, and worked his way through to completion of a solid college career.

Tony muses about his experience, "If I'd looked at the money and decided, 'OK. I can't do this,' I'd still be in Kenya, and I wouldn't have had the opportunity that I've had here. Just take that first step with what you have [and] allow God to direct toward your next step. Let your need be known to those who can help . . . and you will do it."

14

A PHANTOM'S PRAYER

If you own a copy of *The Phantom of the Opera*
(The Complete Original London Cast Recording),
then you know who Michael Crawford is. If you
have witnessed the musical on stage in either
London or New York, you've probably seen
firsthand the power and grace this English actor
brings to the role of the Phantom.

45

If you follow the life of the stage even more
closely, then you know Michael has earned a
number of accolades, including a Tony Award, a
Drama Desk Award, the Dramalogue and Los
Angeles Critics Awards, and the Olivier Award
for Best Actor in a Musical.

Perhaps you didn't know that years before the
world of theatre, music, and film, Michael Crawford
was a lonely twenty-one-year-old sitting in a
church, mourning the loss of his recently deceased
mother.

The days of her death and burial had been especially hard on Michael. The woman who had spent the last two decades looking after him, caring for him, loving him, laughing with him, and crying with him was no more. It was almost too much for Michael to bear.

He found himself back in the church where his mother had often taken him. A sorrowful prayer formed inside him. In the silence of eternity, the young man poured out his grief into the lap of his loving Savior. He didn't expect Jesus to raise his mother from the dead. He really didn't know what to expect. He only knew that he needed to pray.

There was no miracle of resurrection that day, but there was a miracle taking place. While he was praying in the church, Michael felt the comfort of the Holy Spirit washing through him. A sense of peacefulness and understanding replaced the sorrow that had filled his heart. A seed of regeneration, watered by his tears and brought to life by God, had been planted in Michael's heart.

There's a reason for things happening in life, Michael thought to himself. *From this point on I will take what I've been taught by my mother and go on with my life and do good with it.*

Michael felt God speaking to him and felt that his mother would have wanted this. So gathering his courage, he walked out of that church to face the world with confidence found only in God.

15

AIN'T IT GRAND?

Kelly Nelon Thompson, a southern gospel
performer, has recorded over twenty albums and
six videos. Many of her songs have been number
one on the charts. She has appeared on television;
she has performed in sold-out concert halls; she
has won three Grammy Awards and many Dove
Awards; she has won a Gospel Voice Award, a New
York Film Festival Bronze Award, and numerous
Singing News Fan Awards. She also performs on
cruises, at amusement parks, and in local churches.
But Kelly's style is simple. One such tribute is her
rendition of "I Have Decided to Follow Jesus,"
sung in Navajo. Her songs have the capacity to
soften any heart—young, old, fragile, hardened.

But on January 22, 1997, Kelly Nelon
Thompson wasn't caring about her credits. As a
mom, she was desperately worried about her
newborn baby.

She had carried the child during the recording of a new album with her family, The Nelons. She had felt the child kick and move inside her. She and her husband, Jerry, awaited the day they would welcome their baby into the world. The day finally came on January 20, 1997. Two days later doctors discovered a hole in the child's lung, resulting in oxygen-deficient blood. The little life hung in the balance as the baby was placed in intensive care.

Kelly was distraught, filled with emotion and fear. She turned to the only one she knew could help her: Jesus. As she was praying for her child to recover, Kelly thought of a dear family friend and fellow gospel singer, Vestal Goodman. Kelly wished she could spill her heart to Vestal's listening ear; she wished Vestal could be there to pray for the new life God had brought into her family. But Vestal could be anywhere on a gospel tour.

Kelly continued praying and waiting to see how God would respond. Unexpectedly, the phone rang. On the other end was Vestal Goodman, calling to chat with Kelly.

Until the phone call, Vestal had had no idea that Kelly's baby had complications. She simply felt impressed by God to check on her friend, calling around until she'd tracked down Kelly's phone number. Then Vestal prayed for the baby, for Kelly, and for the family.

Two hours later doctors reported a miraculous change in the baby's condition. The hole in the lung was closing itself! By the next day, January 23, the lung was completely healed. With joy, Kelly and Jerry thanked God for healing their child.

16

ALPHABET
DREAMS?

Janice Thatcher woke up with a start. The night
was still dark, but she was wide awake.

DCE. DCE. DCE.

Those three letters kept running through her
mind as if planted there by some subconscious
force. She lay in bed for a few moments, thinking
DCE? What is that?

Janice rolled over and tried to get back to sleep,
but she still felt troubled by her thoughts. Too
many decisions were weighing on her mind.
Among the weighty decisions was where to attend
college next year. Having just completed a two-
year program at a junior college in the San Diego
area, Janice was at a crossroad. It was time to
choose the four-year university where she would
complete her degree—and time to decide what
that degree's focus would be. Shouldn't a junior in

college know by now what she wanted to do with her life?

Janice wasn't sure. She sighed and rolled over again. *DCE. DCE. DCE.* The letters continued to echo in her mind.

Janice had been praying for weeks now, asking God's direction to help her know which major and career to pursue. Honestly, all she wanted to do was serve the Lord in the way he wanted. But what did he want? Janice didn't know, so she prayed each day for God to reveal his will to her.

The frustrated college student started to drift off to sleep once more, then suddenly her eyes flew open.

DCE! she thought.

Wasn't that somewhere on the bulletin board at church? Yes, it was. It was on the flier about Christ College in Irvine, California—a place about an hour north of Janice's San Diego area home. DCE, of course! It stood for "Director of Christian Education." In many Christian denominations, the DCE was the person in charge of the educational ministry of a local church.

Could the director of Christian education be God's direction for me?

With possibilities meandering through her head, Janice dropped off to sleep. The next morning, she sent a letter to Christ College, requesting information about their director of Christian education program. When the proper materials arrived a few weeks later, she knew she had the answer she'd been praying for.

Janice Thatcher enrolled in Christ College and

earned her bachelor's degree in the DCE program. Janice shared what she was learning and practicing in her own church and as an intern in the magazine department at the church resources company, Group Publishing. Before long, Janice became the editor of Group Publishing's *Junior High Ministry* magazine, using her college training to empower thousands of DCEs across the nation in their ministries to America's young people.

17

THE GOATS HEAD
CLUB

Matt, Charlie, Steve, and Dan prayed silently
as they approached the door of the San Francisco
nightclub. They were scheduled to perform there
that night but had second thoughts when they saw
the bouncer standing at the door wearing a T-shirt
that proclaimed, "666 is my favorite number."

The four guys in Jars of Clay (Dan Haseltine,
Steve Mason, Charlie Lowell, and Matt Odmark)
had been praying for an opportunity to use their
music to reach out to unbelievers. They had
pleaded with God—both individually and
collectively—to let them be "bridge builders" and
"ground softeners" who prepare the way for Christ
to come into people's lives. When they received
the invitation to play at the city's party spot by
the bay, they had accepted. And now, despite
reservations, they were determined to go through

with their performance of Jesus-focused songs in the San Francisco hangout.

About an hour before midnight, they walked inside the nightclub and saw a big goat's head—a symbol of Satan worship—prominently displayed above the stage. They laugh about it now, but at the time they weren't sure how to react. Dan says, "We were all pretty naive to the club scene. We didn't know *what* to expect. . . . [The goat's head] showed us that this is *not* a place Christians frequent! I think we were all really scared about how people were going to react to what we were doing and things we were singing."

The guys began their set. Just then, a fight broke out in the back of the bar. Trying to calm their shaking nerves, the four young men continued singing, praying for God's Spirit to take over and bring peace to the room. They sang, and stone-faced drinkers stared back up at them—or simply ignored them altogether. They performed hit tunes like "Love Song for a Savior" and "Flood."

Almost imperceptibly, a hush began to fall over the nightclub. Trickling through the strings, keyboards, and lyrics, the message of the music started penetrating the hearts of those who had previously ignored it. God was present, moving quietly in the club, answering the silent prayers of the band members who had asked to be vehicles of his love to this lost world.

"By the end of the set," Dan says, "the transformation that took place from the beginning of the show to the end of the show was so obvious

. . . just to watch the faces turn from very stone cold, to transparent. It was intense that night."

Steve adds, "We were so afraid, and there were so many variables involved. It was obvious this was one of those places where God wanted us to trust him. . . . We were kind of ill at ease because we knew we were right there where the Word and the world were colliding, and we were watching it happen."

The band reports that new prayers passed their lips—prayers of praise and deeper commitment. "OK, God," Steve remembers praying. "We know this is what you want us to do. You've worked here and shown us that if we're obedient to this calling then you have work to do in these people's lives."

18

INDIANA
PRAYERS

"Heather's desperately ill."

Sandi Stonehill audibly choked back her tears on the phone line. Christian musician Randy Stonehill sank into the hotel-room bed, stunned.

It was November 1982. The man known to his fans as "Uncle Rand" was on the last leg of a concert tour that finished up in Indiana. As was his custom before a concert, he called his wife in Seal Beach, California.

When he called, she gave him the news: Their eight-month-old daughter, Heather, was ill. The physicians had extracted a vial of spinal fluid, and instead of being clear like healthy fluid, it was milky and white. The doctors diagnosed Heather with spinal meningitis.

Sandi continued relating the news to Randy. "They said she could die. If she doesn't die—if she survives it—she could still come out of the experience with retardation or deafness, or muscular problems—any number of things. So we're in bad shape here." She broke off.

The couple ended their conversation. Devastated and in shock, Randy sat on the edge of the bed. A thousand thoughts flooded his mind. He prayed, earnestly seeking God's healing hand. Randy caught himself trying to strike a bargain. "God, if you'll heal Heather, then I'll . . ." But he realized that God didn't need anything Randy had to offer—and that God actually cared about Heather more than he did.

"I realized there was nothing I could do, which is a very helpless, vulnerable feeling," Randy reports today. "But then I realized that God was God, and what I needed to do was trust grace."

Trembling, Randy picked up the phone and called his wife back. "Please don't be angry at me. I think God is telling me to stay and—I don't know how I'm going to get through the show tonight 'cause I'm sort of in shock—but I think I'm supposed to stay and have the audience pray for Heather."

Sandi did not respond angrily, as Randy had expected. "I think you're right. Stay and do the show tonight and call me. And do the show tomorrow night and call me."

There was silence on the line as Sandi composed herself. "There's nothing you can do if you're here. You could sit at her bedside and pray or you can pray in Indiana. God's going to hear you either way. God's going to do what he's going to do."

Though he felt his heart had been ripped out, Randy went onstage that night and performed. During the concert, he paused and enlisted the audience in prayer for his baby daughter. He repeated the request the next night. When Randy entered the plane to go home that third day, all he knew was that Heather wasn't getting better; but she wasn't getting worse.

When Sandi picked up her husband at the airport, her eyes were red but dry. "Doctors don't know what's going on, but Heather's recovering—rapidly!"

Noting Heather's health improvement, the doctors took another sample of spinal fluid. This time the fluid was clearing up! The meningitis was leaving. The puzzled doctors returned to the original milky fluid they'd removed from Heather's spine three days prior. Much to their surprise, the fluid in that vial was miraculously clearing up too—at the same rate that Heather was recovering. As the fluid in the vial progressed, so did Heather. In a short time the vial was clear—and Heather was healed. God had answered those Indiana prayers to the most minute detail.

Sixteen years later, Randy—now the father of a teenager—reports there have been no aftereffects of the disease whatsoever. He still tears up when relating the story of how God healed both his daughter and a vial of fluid, commenting with a grateful smile, "This is how romantic God is."

19

A MEETING
WITH GOD

John Croyle almost didn't stop by that day in
1988, but he was in Pensacola and decided to
visit his friend anyway.

John spent most of his time at the Big Oak
Ranch in Gadsden, Alabama. He and his wife,
Tee, had started the place more than two decades
ago to provide homes for orphaned and abused
children. At Big Oak Ranch, the Croyles have
ministered to over thirteen hundred children who
have grown up there. The Croyles have been
answers to the prayers of others.

But this day John had a prayer of his own. He
had located a piece of property that was perfect for
the new girls' ranch he was hoping to build, but
it cost forty thousand dollars—which was forty
thousand dollars more than Big Oak Ranch could
spare. John felt strongly that God was leading him
to buy this land, so he made it a matter of prayer.

He outlined the need to God, then asked him to provide the means to purchase the property.

On his business trip to Pensacola, John visited his friend, a man who was a successful and busy attorney. Little did John know that God was about to arrange an important meeting through that visit.

John entered the friend's office and greeted him warmly. The lawyer returned the greeting, then asked curiously, "What are you working on now?"

"Well, I'm trying to put together a girls' ranch. There's one piece of property that's going to cost us forty thousand dollars. . . ."

Before he could finish, the phone rang. On the other end of the line was the lawyer's partner. "What are you doing?"

Smiling at John, the lawyer in the office answered, "Well, I'm sitting here talking with John Croyle about this girls' ranch he's wanting to build and this piece of property."

"What's he want?" the partner asked.

"Forty thousand dollars."

Without hesitating, the partner said, "You do half; I'll do half."

When John's friend immediately agreed, John realized that his prayer had been answered affirmatively.

Ninety seconds later John Croyle walked out of the lawyer's office with forty thousand dollars to buy that piece of property. He would build that girls' ranch after all!

Looking back on that experience, John still marvels at God's timing. God had put it in John's mind to visit the friend and then convened a phone meeting with the two lawyers right on the spot.

"That's big-boy stuff!" John comments today, adding, "There's no such thing as a little miracle. They're all big."

20

INTERVIEW
WITH A KILLER

It was probably when the killer sat down in front
of him at that Florida prison that Bill first thought,
What in the world am I doing here? Swallowing his
discomfort, Bill proceeded with the interview. He
had to. It was an answer to a prayer he had prayed
years before.

As a collegian at the University of Washington,
Bill had taken a course in writing. The Cs and Ds
he earned on assignments in that class soon
convinced him he was not cut out for that line
of work.

Twenty years old at the time, Bill approached
God with a prayer: "Lord, I'll do anything for you
that you want me to. Except write, of course."

Following God's leading, Bill changed his major
to stage directing and earned a degree from the
university. He traveled to Italy, adding filmmaking
to his studies, and completed his coursework at the

Italian State Institute of Cinema in Rome. Bill attacked the avenues of stage and screen with a passion. Returning to the United States, he acted and directed, using his gifts and talents on a variety of stage and film productions.

Then one day a publisher approached Bill and asked him to write a book. He thought about turning it down—after all, he had made poor grades on many of his college papers. But the prayer he prayed as a twenty-year-old still echoed in his heart: *Lord, I'll do anything for you that you want me to. . . .* Maybe it was time for Bill to drop the *except* from that prayer. Did God want him to write? Bill accepted the opportunity.

More than forty books and two dozen screenplays later, Bill Myers is still writing. He's received over forty national and international awards for his work. He authored and cocreated the video series McGee & Me! Each of these videos has sold over 2 million copies. Related book sales total 450,000 copies. Additionally, he's sold over a million copies of other Christian books for children and youth. He is the author of Christian thriller novels for adults like *Threshold* and *Blood of Heaven*.

It was his research for *Blood of Heaven* that brought him face-to-face with a convicted murderer in the Florida prison. The premise of the book was a game of "What if . . ." that explored the changes a hardened criminal might experience if he received a sample of Christ's DNA. Bill felt it would be important to research his novel to the fullest extent—which meant visits to genetic labs as well as prisons.

Bill was determined to be present for that interview with a killer. He had to. It was one of many answers to a prayer he had constantly prayed.

21

GOD
AT THE GRAMMYS?

If you watched the 1996 Grammy Awards, you
remember that a highlight of the show was when
Christian singer CeCe Winans performed a gospel
segment with mainstream singer Whitney Houston.
A standing ovation erupted at the end of that portion
of the show, with Christians and non-Christians
alike touched by the Spirit of God through the
performance. But CeCe Winans originally wasn't
even scheduled to perform. The show's organizers
had decided against including a gospel segment.

However, CeCe didn't believe them. During
her prayer time, she felt God strongly encouraging
her to pray for her performance at the Grammys.
She knew she wasn't scheduled to sing but prayed
to that end anyway. "It's almost like God put it in
my spirit [that] it was going to happen before it
happened. And I just began to pray on it and ask
the Lord to magnify or to let it be an explosion.

Let it be something that people will remember and will remember him in."

Then she waited—but not for long. She chuckles. "All of a sudden, things just started happening. God started working in the minds and the hearts of men. And Whitney called me, and she said, 'CeCe, they're only going to do a gospel singing if I'm a part of a gospel segment.' I was like, 'Oh, really?' And right then I knew God had started working."

The two singers began planning for the newly installed gospel segment of the show. They would start off with the duet they had recorded, "Count on Me," but then what? CeCe made it a matter of prayer once more and felt God was leading her to sing "I Surrender All." But that was a mellow song, a plain old hymn from days gone by. Would the director go for that one?

With a twinkle in her eye, CeCe reports that soon after, "The musical director called and said, 'CeCe, what do you want to do? I was thinking about "I Surrender All."'" And I said, 'Yeah, that would be good.' So it's like all through that whole planning thing, I was just like, 'God, you are tripping me out!'"

In a matter of days, the show had gone from no-gospel-segment-and-no-CeCe Winans to straight-up-gospel-with-CeCe Winans and Whitney Houston!

When it came time to perform, CeCe gratefully remembers, "Before we went on, I prayed. I was like, 'Lord, I'm not here for myself. It's not about me. It's all about you. You anoint this thing.' And the power that came in that place was just incredible!"

22

THE GRINNING PASTOR

Max grinned in his office at the little Florida
church where he was an associate pastor. He was
really enjoying himself.

He paused for a moment, then typed out the
next sentence for his column in the church
bulletin. Creating this column was part of his
pastoral responsibilities at the Central Church of
Christ in Miami, Florida. He knew this would
only go out to the people in his church, but he
gave it his all anyway. That wasn't difficult to do,
for he really enjoyed putting together those short
pieces for the congregation.

The congregation enjoyed the pieces too. "You
should try to get these published!" many exclaimed
each week when a new bulletin came out. Max
would smile, shake his head and say, "Well, maybe
. . . and maybe not!"

After two years at Central Church, Max was

approved to pursue his dream of being a missionary to South America. With warm farewells from his congregation, he packed his things and moved to Brazil to spread the good news of Jesus there.

He arrived in Rio de Janeiro, Brazil. He immediately plunged into a crash course in Portuguese, doing the best he could to learn the new language so he could communicate with those in the mission field. Still, in the back of his mind he heard the words of the Miami church about his articles in the bulletin: "You should try to get these published!"

A seed had been planted, and Max began to pray, asking God to help him decide whether or not to pursue publication of his weekly musings. Although his days were filled with studying Portuguese verbs and nouns and dialect, his evenings were almost always free. During those evenings in Brazil, he pulled out his past columns and worked to compile them into a coherent manuscript.

Max continued to pray through the writing; then he sent out his new manuscript to a publisher. He waited weeks for an answer. When the letter came, it was a rejection notice. The publisher wasn't interested in what Max had to offer.

Could this be God's answer? Max wondered. He thought about giving up, but deep inside he felt God urging him to send the book to another publisher. So he did. . . .

And got another rejection letter.

Max sent his manuscript to fourteen Christian publishers and received fourteen different rejection letters. The fifteenth publisher on Max's list was Tyndale House Publishers in Illinois. He mailed his book one last time. . . .

And this time Max Lucado's first book was accepted. Published with the title *On the Anvil*, it began his professional writing career.

Since then, Max Lucado has written *No Wonder They Call Him the Savior*, *In the Grip of Grace*, *When God Whispers Your Name*, and *Just Like Jesus*, among other books. His books have sold over 5 million copies. His lyrical writing style has earned him several awards, including two Gold Medallion Christian Book of the Year Awards. During the 1990s his books were often among the best-sellers. He has much to offer to twentieth- and twenty-first century Christians.

Max chuckles when remembering his start as a writer. *"[On the Anvil]* is actually the only book I've ever done with Tyndale. But it was the first one, and I've always been thankful to the Tyndale people for publishing it."

23

COLLEGE
CONFUSION

Junior college student Jim Gray was out-and-out
confused. He was hardly able to make sense of
anything. An overwhelming amount of financial-
aid paperwork was the source of his dilemma.

"It seemed like every other day in the mail I
was receiving something that I had to sign for
some kind of loan or whatnot. And with all the
different loans and grants and scholarships that are
available, it's really confusing."

Although he was bewildered by the financial-aid
process, he felt certain about one thing: God was
leading him to transfer out of junior college and
continue his studies at Anderson University in
Anderson, Indiana.

"I'd planned on transferring to Syracuse
University . . . and that all changed. Through
prayer and conversation with God, I got the calling
to go into youth ministry; Anderson kept popping

up. I felt that if God really wanted me to go there, he was going to provide for me."

Though confused, Jim determined to tackle the maze of forms and applications before him. He enlisted the help of independent financial-aid counselor C. K. Dykstra. "There was a lot of frustration," Jim remembers, "knowing that money was there somewhere but not knowing how to get to it through all the red tape and stuff. [C. K. Dykstra] helped me get through that."

Dykstra not only helped Jim fill out the forms line by line, but he also gave sound advice to help Jim make paying for school a priority.

Jim laughs when he recalls one conversation with Dykstra. "'Don't be spending!' he said to me. 'Now's not the time to blow the money you're making. You need to save your money.' That's something I had a hard time with. [But now] I really wish I would have saved more money!"

Dykstra also encouraged Jim to be willing to work to help pay his own way—even if it meant scrubbing dorm toilets and cleaning classroom desks through the college work-study program. Jim worked as a janitor through college, earning the nickname "Janitor Jim" from his classmates.

With financial-aid forms out of the way, Jim knew he had to make the biggest investment he could toward school—an investment in prayer.

"I prayed that if God wanted me [here] that he would make it possible."

Jim also recruited several youth leaders at his church to pray specifically for his school finances because "the financial part of it was the only thing that was going to hold me back." The youth leaders held occasional prayer meetings in their homes, asking God to provide money for Jim's schooling.

Jim's investments paid off when he sat down in the Financial Aid Office of Anderson University to go over his aid package. He found that the aid was enough.

Reflecting on that meeting, Jim smiles. "When I saw that financial-aid package, I was ecstatic about it. That was an answer to prayer."

24

REDEEMING
PRAYER

Rob Anderson held the letter in his hand and
smiled. He read it again, then folded it up and put
it in a safe place. He had to keep this one. It was
an answer to prayer.

Rob remembered the day when he started
praying his prayer. A successful game designer who
had helped create Scattergories and Catch the
Mouse, Rob turned an eye toward the games that
were being created for teenagers. What he found
were dark fantasy/adventure games: Dungeons and
Dragons; Magic: The Gathering; and Vampire:
The Eternal Struggle.

That was when the prayer began to form in his
heart. "Lord, help me to create a morally positive
alternative to these games. Help me to create a game
for teenagers that will draw them closer to you."

Making that his constant prayer, Rob set to
work. Adopting the trading card method of Magic:

The Gathering, he designed a fantasy/adventure game for teenagers based on biblical themes.

Carefully crafting the game, Rob decided that the quest would be to win lost souls. The "heroes" would be godly men and women found in the pages of the Bible. The "villains" would reflect real-life characters whose prototypes are mentioned in Scripture. To help them win lost souls, players would be armed with Bible-based "enhancement" cards, and even a few "miraculous" power cards. Because each player could choose the cards that go into his or her own deck, no two decks would be exactly the same.

With the craft finished, Rob hired the finest artists available to create illustrations for the cards. He called his new game Redemption and released it in the summer of 1995. A year and a half later, a quarter million decks of the game had been sold. Redemption tournaments cropped up in schools, and in some areas youth groups were playing Redemption every week. The Redemption worldwide championship takes place each year.

But what really made it all worthwhile for Rob was the letter. It was the first letter he'd received from a fan of the game, a young man who was then a sophomore in college.

This teenager had been raised in a Christian home but had abandoned his faith while away at school. He had also become involved in playing several unhealthy, role-playing fantasy games. Along the way, someone introduced him to Redemption. God began convicting him with the gospel message of the game and the Scriptures found on each card. Before long, he had thrown out the dark fantasy games and recommitted his life to Jesus. He wrote Rob Anderson to tell him about it.

"I think that will stand out in my mind above anything else," Anderson says today. "Now, I've gotten other letters since then from kids who have gotten out of the dark and horrific games, and they've started reading their Bibles or walking closer with the Lord. But I think the first one that I got was probably the most memorable. It was so exciting!"

25

MORE LIKE
A WHISPER

To be honest, Joyce Martin McCollough was ready
to leave. As one-third of the award-winning southern
gospel trio the Martins, Joyce had gathered with her
siblings at their record company's office building to
preview new songs in hopes of finding a few for their
new album.

Looking back on that day of listening to songs
in Phil Johnson's office, big sister Joyce admits,
"We were not really in the best of moods. And we
were not really agreeing about song selection and
all that."

Eventually Phil said, "I have one more song to
play you." He cued up a song written by Scott
Krippayne and Steve Siler called "More Like a
Whisper."

Judy Martin Hess, the "little sis," wasn't
listening all that closely either. She and Joyce
almost let this song pass by. Then she noticed

Jonathan, the brother in the middle of the two girls, weeping quietly as he listened. Judy and Joyce immediately tuned in to the song.

The lyrics of the chorus rang out, "When questions rain down like thunder, sometimes the answer is more like a whisper. . . ."

With tears rolling down his face as the song ended, Jonathan said, "That makes me think about Taylor."

Taylor Martin, Jonathan's son and the nephew of Joyce and Judy, was born as a twin with his brother, Michael, on New Year's Eve, 1995. Jonathan and his wife, Melinda, were thrilled to welcome the boys into the world. But they were worried since the twins weren't expected until March 1996.

Born two-and-a-half months premature, both babies struggled at birth, and doctors weren't sure either would survive. Family and friends prayed, and somehow the boys gained strength and were allowed to go home healthy. No one knew anything was still wrong with Taylor until just over a year later, February 1997.

Michael had begun sitting up and crawling and doing all the things babies do, but Taylor still was not progressing in his development. Tests revealed that Taylor had brain damage—the crippling disease cerebral palsy.

Jonathan and Melinda, along with their extended families and friends, immediately began praying for healing, asking God to restore health to this child. In concert after concert across the country, Jonathan shared about his sons and requested prayer for Taylor. Deep inside Jonathan hoped for a miracle of the mountain-moving kind. He wanted his child to be completely transformed by the healing power of God.

But sometimes miracles don't come in that shape and size. Sometimes they're more like a whisper.

When Taylor was around eighteen months old, he did something doctors weren't sure he'd ever do. He began to speak.

Yes, he still had cerebral palsy. Yes, he was still unable to walk. Yes, he still had difficulty moving his lower body and his arms. But he did begin to speak.

Jonathan states, "He says, 'Dada,' and 'Mama,' and 'Papa.' But he also says the name of Jesus, which is for us a very, very special thing."

If Taylor is able to speak, then it's possible he will walk and grow and eventually be able to live a normal life, despite his disability. Taylor's voice became a whispered answer to Jonathan's prayer, a breath of hope.

Jonathan explains, "God didn't just heal Taylor, but through Taylor improving and starting to speak, it was that little one-and-a-half-year-old voice speaking 'Daddy' and saying 'Jesus' and saying 'I love you,' confirmed in my heart that 'Hey! This is your answer. This is God saying everything's going to be all right.'"

Back in the record company's office, Judy said to Phil Johnson, "We've got to listen to that one again." Phil cued up the tape of "More Like a

Whisper" once more. When the song ended this time, there wasn't a dry eye in the room.

"More Like a Whisper" made the album. You can hear it on the Martins' CD, *Dream Big*. If you're a fan of the Martins, you'll notice something special about this song on the album. The trio opted not to sing it in their trademarked three-part harmony style. Jonathan sings it solo, telling the world that sometimes God's answer to prayer is more like a whisper.

26

STAGE
FRIGHT!

By the time she was seventeen years old, Nikki
Leonti had already released her debut album,
Shelter Me—a CD that immediately rode up the
charts to a slot in *CCM Update*'s top-five Christian
albums and earned a place in the top twelve on the
Billboard charts. She has also toured the nation
singing her lively brand of pop music.

When Nikki confidently takes the stage for a
show, she fears little when it comes to singing. She
loves to sing—it comes easily. But when it comes to
talking, Nikki's confidence fades a little. Performing
for an audience comes more naturally than sharing
about her life in front of them.

"I had a problem talking when I sang or did a
concert. I always knew what I wanted and needed
to say to people, but I had a fear that they would
think I sounded juvenile. I also wanted the courage
to talk about past circumstances, such as [when]

my six-year-old brother died of cancer. . . . I wanted to share about that, but I never knew how to word it."

For concert after concert, Nikki would sail through her songs with ease, then stumble over her words when it came time to speak. She knew something had to be done.

Nikki turned to the one who created her mouth, who blessed her with the talent to sing. She prayed, asking Jesus to give her courage to share and wisdom to speak the words that others needed to hear. She felt certain that in each audience there might be at least one person who would be helped by hearing how Jesus had brought her through trials and hard times in her life. She prayed for God to help her overcome her stage fright and for God to use her words to minister to those who came to hear her sing.

During March 1998, Nikki stood onstage. She did not know that a hurting young man was sitting in the audience that day. The man's brother was fighting a losing battle against cancer. The man felt helpless and discouraged knowing that his brother would soon die, but he didn't know what to do about it.

Neither Nikki nor the young man could have guessed that they shared this experience. But in between songs, Nikki felt God's strength flowing through her as she shared a bit of her testimony with the audience. She spoke of the despair she felt when her brother passed away and of how Christ had brought her through that time.

The young man sat deep in thought, realizing

he was not alone. After the concert, he sought Nikki out and shared his experience with her. The two young people prayed together, thanked God that he had brought them to this place at this time, and asked God for strength and healing in the days to come.

Afterward Nikki thought about how things might have been different if God hadn't answered her prayer or given her the courage to speak about her life. That young man might have walked away never knowing that Jesus could carry him through times of trouble.

Today Nikki rejoices that God continues to answer her prayer for courage. She rarely struggles with stage fright anymore. "Now I share [my] testimony at every concert. And at least one person in the audience will be going through the same thing. I've learned now to open up and share what the Lord is leading me to say."

27

ELEVEN ANGRY
COMMISSIONERS

It was like a scene from the movie *Twelve Angry Men*. In that classic film, Henry Fonda plays the part of a juror who stands alone in his conviction that a defendant is not guilty.

This time, however, there were only eleven decision makers in the room. They had been assigned to the Attorney General's Commission on Pornography. The year was 1986, and the commission had just voted ten to one in favor of releasing a report that did *not* classify pornography as harmful to individuals, families, and society at large.

Dr. James Dobson, founder of the Christian organization Focus on the Family, had cast the sole dissenting vote. The commission had spent the past year and a half studying and debating the effects of pornography on the nation. At the end of the process, only Dr. Dobson believed in pornography's detrimental effects on people.

The commission was about to come to a close. The final week was upon them; everyone looked forward to walking out of their Washington, D.C., meeting room and stepping back into their everyday lives. Then came Wednesday's vote. Dr. Dobson voted to classify pornography as harmful in the commission's report. The ten other members voted against him.

Thousands of miles away, at the Focus on the Family offices then located in southern California, Dr. Dobson's staff received news of the vote's outcome. Only two days remained before the commission was to dismiss. What could they do to help?

Noontime at Focus headquarters was an unusual sight. Three hundred employees streamed into the organization's parking lot, choosing to give up their lunchtime for corporate prayer. They asked God to allow the truth about pornography to be revealed through the commission. They prayed that Dr. Dobson might be firm in his stance against pornography. They asked for a miracle to occur in the hearts and minds of the members of the commission. When the lunch hour was over, the staff returned to their work, not knowing if their prayers had made a difference.

Thursday morning in Washington, D.C., the attorney general's Commission on Pornography assembled as planned. Unexpectedly, one of Dr. Dobson's opponents asked to speak. Although he had previously demonstrated a liberal approach to pornography, he stunned everyone by telling them he had changed his mind. Now, he saw pornography as a complex moral issue instead of a slight educational one. He proceeded to give an impassioned speech in favor of Dr. Dobson's position, completely reversing his view—and his vote—from the prior day.

Several of the commissioners nodded their heads. They, too, changed their vote as the discussion continued into Friday—the last day of the commission. The final report issued by these commissioners stated very clearly that pornography is both immoral and dangerous.

Reflecting on that tenuous, yet rewarding, week, Dr. Dobson had only one explanation. "The entire situation changed in a matter of two days. Why? Because three hundred people were fasting and praying."

28

FINDING GOD
ON THE RESERVATION

Between 9:00 P.M. and 10:00 P.M. on September
19, 1997, forty-one-year-old Rich Mullins was
tragically killed in an automobile accident. The
man who had written the songs "Awesome God"
and "Creed" (which is a musical recitation of the
Apostles' Creed) no longer lived on earth.

The Christian community mourned,
remembering the uniqueness of Rich's life and
musical vision. For some years Rich had been a
schoolteacher on a Navajo reservation in New
Mexico, where he taught music to the junior
highers. His decision to invest his life in Native
American children came as an answer to prayer.

During a trip to Asia several years before his
death, Rich was able to view Christianity from the
perspective of a completely different culture. The
result was life-changing for him. "I got to go to
Asia for the summer. It was a great opportunity for

me to see Christianity from a non-twentieth-century, American slant. What that did for me was confirm the truth of the essence of Christianity, and it challenged my opinions about peripheral issues."

When Rich returned to the U.S., the idea of living out his faith in a different culture appealed to him. But family and financial constraints prevented him from returning to Asia. He prayed, asking God for the opportunity to live, work, and reach out to others in the context of a different culture. He prayed for God's direction and asked that God show him how and where to go. Rich desperately wanted to follow God in the matter.

After a time the answer became clear, and he didn't have to travel far to see it. He found different cultures right in the heart of the U.S. "Here in this country we have some two hundred cultures that are *not* white-Anglo-Saxon-Protestant-twentieth-century-evangelical-Christian."

Certain he was following God's direction, he went back to school, earned a degree in music education, then moved to the Navajo reservation in New Mexico to live, teach, and make music within the Navajo culture. "I came here [to the Navajo reservation] hoping to once again include in my vision the slant that these people have."

29

RIGHT OFF
THE COLLEGE

"A musician's nightmare . . . So horribly uncomfortable. So naked." The voice on the phone winces audibly. The Christian artist Eli remembers struggling as a musician.

On the night before Thanksgiving, Eli found himself prepping for a show at a Penn State University coffee shop called "Right Off the College." Fresh off a few dates at big venues with large crowds, Eli was ready. . . .

Until show time, when he realized the audience that evening would be a paltry seven people.

"You stand in front of a hundred people, you can do no wrong," Eli comments. "It's easy to stand in front of a thousand people because you can smile and they go, 'Yeah!' You sit down and they go, 'Yeah!' But when you get in front of [seven] people like that . . . you'd better have something to say."

Eli felt like leaving, but instead, he decided to pray. Silently he asked God to bless the concert and to be present in the music and the message. Inside he wrestled with nervousness, but he knew God had arranged the situation. Perhaps one of those seven kids really needed to hear what Eli had to share. Maybe it would somehow encourage one person to draw closer to Christ.

Eli prayed that God would use him that night, no matter how few people showed up. Then Eli did what he does best: "We sang songs, and I ministered to them." He shared his faith and how Jesus had rescued him from an addiction to alcohol and drugs, making him a new creature inside and out.

After the concert most of the students went their separate ways to prepare for the Thanksgiving holiday. One student hesitated, however, and made his way up to the artist.

"Man," he said, "I just became a Christian thirty days ago. I've been clean [sober] for thirty days. Thank you so much."

The words of Eli's testimony and the lyrics of his songs had reached out and touched this one student, encouraging a new Christian to pursue a deeper relationship with Christ. The student and the artist lingered during the cold November evening, warming the night with conversation and prayer together. If more people had been in the audience, it's possible the young man might have skipped the chance to chat with Eli. Or perhaps, if he hadn't found a seat, he might have left the show altogether. Two years later Eli smiles when he remembers that encounter.

30

MOM'S
LITTLE PROJECT

Karyn looked up and down the aisle again, then shook her head and picked up a book. A mother of both a preschooler and a toddler, all she wanted was a Bible storybook to read to her children. But since she was also a trained teacher with a specialty in early childhood, she knew what was—and wasn't—appropriate for young minds.

She returned the book to the shelf. That one wouldn't work—too babyish for her preschooler. Skimming the shelves at the Christian bookstore, she reached for another story Bible and quickly put it down again. The pictures were cute, but the text was way over a little child's head.

Karyn sighed. She hadn't expected it to be this difficult to find a resource for sharing the Bible with her kids. She took one last look at the books that lined the store's shelves. She made a decision and left empty-handed. At this point, no story Bible was a better choice than a poorly done one.

At home, Karyn regaled her two sons with other stories from a set of books she'd ordered through the mail. These books also came with read-along tapes, and her children loved them! The delightful stories reached her kids right where they were, capturing the boys' imagination while teaching a life lesson.

Why not have Bible stories produced in a set like this? Karyn thought in frustration. She wanted to give up but instead pursued her thoughts and turned to God for help.

God, please give me guidance and help me make this dream a reality, she prayed as an idea brewed in her head. That prayer became a constant plea from Karyn during the months that followed, and she began a task many Bible publishers had ignored.

Opening her own adult Bible and recruiting her husband, Ralph, to help with development, Karyn started "translating" stories of the Scripture into language appropriate for—and entertaining to—preschoolers. Before long, the work took on a life of its own as Karyn carefully scripted each scene, even adding her own illustrations to help visualize the text.

"In the beginning the earth was empty. Darkness covered everything. But God was there, and He had a plan . . . ," began Karyn's retelling of the creation story from Genesis.

Slowly but surely Karyn worked, eventually "translating" ninety-five stories from the Bible for children. She quickly had two avid fans in her sons. They thought hearing Mom's new stories was great! Before long, she had another fan, a friend who offered to market the stories for her. At that point, she recruited another friend, Dennas Davis, to illustrate her stories.

Together, Karyn Henley and Dennas Davis put together a series of sixteen paperback Bible story-books and tapes for kids that they called Dovetales. Those little books were later compiled into one hardcover book just the right size for little hands and renamed *The Beginner's Bible*.

Since that time, Karyn Henley's book has sold over 3 million copies and has been translated into seventeen different languages. The story Bible has inspired CDs, other books, puzzles, and games for children. You may even have a copy of Karyn's book in your child's library!

Reflecting on the time she spent writing *The Beginner's Bible*, Karyn recalls feeling dependent on God for help and direction. "I was always seeking God and yielding the project to him for inspiration and skill. After all, it's his original work!"

31

LET IT RAIN . . .
PLEASE?

If you enjoy a good medical thriller, chances are
you've already discovered Harry Lee Kraus Jr. A
physician by trade, he works as a Christian novelist
on the side. His fiction titles include *Fated Genes*
and *Stainless Steel Hearts*.

But in 1968 Harry played soccer during recess
as a boisterous fourth-grader. He ran, kicked,
skidded, blocked, shouted, and generally enjoyed
himself out on the school's playground.

Then, after an unexpected collision, Harry got
up limping. The pain in his leg told him he must
have taken a hard knock. He hobbled to the
sidelines for the rest of recess; when the bell rang,
he joined his buddies as they all made their way
back to the classroom.

The pain in his leg worsened as the day went
on. If he had been a doctor back then, he would've
quickly diagnosed the problem: a fractured tibia. But

Harry was still too young to know he'd broken his leg. He just knew that it hurt badly.

After school, the pain from the injury was so great he couldn't put any weight on his foot. He was unable to walk. Although the school's staff neglected to call Harry's parents to inform them of the accident, a teacher was kind enough to help him climb carefully into the school bus for the daily ride home.

There Harry sat, a fourth-grader with a broken leg, waiting for the bus to take him to his assigned stop. Feeling the pain, he quickly realized he would not be able to walk the quarter mile from the bus stop to his home. Worried and hurting, Harry thought to pray.

He knew that if it was raining, his mother would drive to pick him up so he would not have to walk home in the wet weather. That's what he prayed for. "God, please send rain so my mother will pick me up." He waited nervously as the bus rumbled through the streets toward his assigned stop.

He checked the sky. It was a clear afternoon, but he kept praying.

Suddenly, out of nowhere, a dark cloud emerged and poured rain all over the city! Until that moment, there had been no indication of a storm.

The bus arrived at Harry's stop, and Harry saw his mother waiting patiently in the car. Gratefully, Harry hobbled down the steps into his mother's car. His mother took him to a doctor, who treated the broken leg, giving relief to the suffering boy.

Harry remembers that sudden cloudburst that prompted his mother to be in just the right spot at just the right time. "I knew God had answered my prayer then. And I believe it now."

32

A TEN-DOLLAR BAG
OF DOG FOOD

"Phil, we're out of dog food."

Lisa Vischer hated having to tell her husband that.

It was 1993 and he was working so hard, praying so hard to make his vision a reality. All he wanted to do was tell stories that would improve kids' lives. He wanted to create an animated series that would use vegetables to teach Judeo-Christian values. Phil possessed creative talent. Phil and his buddy, Mike Nawrocki, were already making high-quality products for children.

The only problem was, nobody wanted them.

Phil had approached several Christian publishers with his idea, explaining his vision, showing samples and mock-ups. None of the publishers expressed an interest in his products.

So Phil became his own producer. Taking part-time commercial work to support his family, he plunged into the grinding legwork needed to bring to life his big idea. In fact, he even named his fledgling company that—Big Idea Productions.

Phil contacted just about everyone he knew for start-up capital. His parents took out a second mortgage on their house and gave the money to Big Idea. His sister invested her toddler's college money in the company. Friends from the Vischers' Bible-study group pulled their retirement funds from the bank and loaned them to Phil. The support was overwhelming. In July of 1993, Phil and Mike gratefully set up shop in a small storefront on the north side of Chicago and started producing their first animated video for kids.

Then, unexpectedly, Phil's commercial work ended. Phil and Mike were still producing the video series, and without other projects on the side, Phil had no way to provide for his family— for his wife, two-year-old daughter, and, of course, the family dog.

Phil prayed long and desperately. He asked God for guidance. He pleaded with God to provide for his family while he finished the Big Idea production.

Little by little the family's money trickled away right up until the night Phil discovered they were down to their last ten dollars. That was it. The extent of their monetary holdings was a single ten-dollar bill tucked away in Phil's wallet.

And the dog was out of food, which cost exactly ten dollars.

Reluctantly, Phil handed the bill to his wife and sent Lisa to the store for more dog food. Phil Vischer was officially broke.

Alone and bewildered, Phil wrestled with God in prayer. *Maybe this crazy idea wasn't God's will after all,* he thought. *Maybe it's time to give up.*

He prayed for a while. Then, to distract himself, he thumbed through the day's mail that lay on the table in front of him. Mixed in the pile was a plain-looking envelope with no return address. Curious, Phil opened the letter and read this anonymous note: "God laid it on my heart that you might need this."

Attached was a cashier's check for four hundred dollars.

Phil recalls, "It couldn't have been any clearer if God himself had walked into our apartment and said, 'I'm right here with you. Just keep going.' The battle I was fighting for the hearts and minds of our kids was his, not mine. I have never doubted it since."

Phil Vischer and Mike Nawrocki went on to complete their first video—and more. They called that first video *Where's God When I'm S-scared* and named their series VeggieTales. To date, VeggieTales has sold over 3 million copies; Big Idea Productions employs around fifty people full time.

And that first video? Recently, it was the number two kids' video in the entire United States, outselling every Barney video, every Rugrats video, every Arthur video, and others snapped up daily in our nation.

Not bad for a guy who could barely afford to buy a bag of dog food, but easy for a God who knew just how—and when—to answer Phil Vischer's prayer.

33

FIVE-YEAR-OLD
HEADACHES

"Daddy, my head hurts!"

Eddie Elguera's heart went out to his five-year-old son, but try as he might, this caring Dad couldn't seem to bring relief to his child's ailment.

True, Eddie could do many things. For starters, he'd been a two-time national skateboarding champion, performing wonders on his board. Now retired from skating, Eddie worked different kinds of wonders, sharing Christ with teenagers as a youth pastor in southern California.

But when his middle son started having recurring headaches in 1992, Eddie was at a loss. Nothing he could do would bring relief for long. He and his wife took the boy to the doctor, but the physician couldn't find the problem either.

"Maybe it's his sinuses," the medical expert suggested. But none of their treatments made the headaches go away.

Eddie checked his son into Loma Linda Hospital. They were going to run tests and find out what the problem was. The hospital staff did CT-scans and physical examinations, running a full battery of tests on the child. But in the end, the doctors came up empty-handed. They couldn't find anything that would cause the massive headaches the poor boy endured.

Through it all, Eddie and his wife prayed. They pleaded with God to bring relief to their son. They asked the Great Physician to locate the problem and heal it. They knew that when the medical world was at a loss, God was just getting started.

The kindergartner checked out of the hospital no different than when he went in. Eddie brought his boy home and, knowing there was nothing doctors could do to help, prayed all the more fervently for God to intervene. After all, God was a Father too, and he knew what it felt like to have a child who was hurting.

At first nothing seemed to change. The headaches came and went as usual. Then one day Eddie noticed that his son had stopped complaining of pain in his head. No, he wasn't hiding the pain—he just wasn't feeling it anymore. As abruptly as the headaches came, they seemed to disappear.

Eddie waited for the headaches to return, through the end of 1992 and into the beginning of 1993. When 1994 rolled around, Eddie's son still hadn't had another headache. At last check, more than five years later, the child remained headache-free.

Eddie testifies to God's goodness. "We just

prayed and believed and went to my pastor at the church. And just prayed and believed. We just know that God healed him. The headaches went away."

34

FUNNY
BUSINESS

Jonathan Slocumb had a problem. A Christian who was also a gifted young comedian, he was praying for a way to break into the comedy circuit.

When Jonathan heard about the Redd Foxx Comedy Search, he thought perhaps that was the answer to his prayer. He decided to enter—and was determined to win.

That was his problem. All the other prominent comedians he knew seemed to get their laughs by lacing their monologues with cursing and obscenity. A self-proclaimed "skinny church boy," Jonathan was not fluent in the language of profanity and was unsure of what to do.

His desire to fit in and win overruled his conscience. "I had never done this before," he recalls, "but I wrote my material out and asked one of my best friends to read it and then write in some curse words where he thought it should be appropriate. So he did, and then I memorized it [for the contest]."

The strategy seemed to work, as Jonathan kept passing the qualifying rounds. In the end Jonathan Slocumb won, tying for first place with another comic. But for Jonathan it was a hollow victory.

God was answering Jonathan's prayer but in a way Jonathan hadn't expected. He was allowing Jonathan to experience the emptiness that comes with success outside of God's will. He was challenging him to live up to a higher standard in his career goals—the God standard.

"I've never been so uncomfortable in my whole life," Jonathan admits. "In fact, I felt like a member of the KKK standing up at the NAACP with his robe on!"

Even as he was posing for his championship picture with Redd Foxx, the Holy Spirit was working on Jonathan's heart. "I said right then, 'I'll never do this again.'

"I knew I was doing wrong, but I thought, *I'll just do it.* But after I won it, I said, 'I believe I can do this without [cursing]. In fact, I know it. . . .' And that was it. Been going straight up ever since."

Over twelve years later Jonathan's prayer for success and God's humbling response keep him busy. Taking his material from the "holy humor" found inside church walls, Jonathan Slocumb's clean comedy has won an audience of both Christians and non-Christians.

He's performed acts on television spots as different as the Christian talk show *The 700 Club* and HBO's gutter-dwelling *Def Comedy Jam*. He's shared the stage with well-known artists like The Winans, Take 6, Kirk Franklin, Aretha Franklin, Natalie Cole, and Toni Braxton, and counts among his fans the heavyweight champion boxer Evander Holyfield and the comedy heavyweight Sinbad.

Jonathan has no plans for slowing down. Because of that, prayer still plays a big part in this comedian's life. "I've learned that you can communicate with God all through the course of the day. I mean, as much as you want to or, sometimes, as little as you want to, knowing that he got the message the first time. So . . . I'm in constant communication with the Lord. I don't think that I can move without him!"

35

GOD
CALLING?

Gina Brown already had one man in her life, but
she was praying for another. Being a single parent
was not an easy job.

Married as a teenager, Gina had her first child
at the age of nineteen. A beautiful little boy, she
named him Corey. Unfortunately, Gina's marriage
deteriorated, quickly becoming an abusive—and
dangerous—situation. As such, the marriage ended
in divorce before Gina's twenty-second birthday.

Newly divorced and struggling to survive, Gina
tried to carve out a new life for herself and her son.
Whenever Corey laughed, gave Gina a hug, or
brightened up a room just by entering it, Gina
knew it was worth it all—all the heartache, all the
hard times, everything. Gina would pause to pray
and thank God for this precious gift.

Still, as much as she enjoyed life with Corey,
she couldn't deny the longing within her to be

loved and treasured by a husband. She wanted a godly man who would put Christ first in his life and who wouldn't get messed up on drugs and become violent. She wanted someone to enter her life to be both a godly husband and a Christlike daddy for Corey.

Gina made that her constant prayer, asking God to bring just the right man into her world. She prayed God would bring that man at just the right time and that he would be all she hoped for.

But, of course, men like that don't come calling every day . . . or do they?

Ellejandro Patrick sat with his headset on and prepared for the next call. It was the 1995 holiday season, and Ellejandro was looking for a way to make a little extra money to spend on Christmas gifts. When he heard about the job at the telemarketing firm, he applied for it and got it. Now he was cold-calling person after person, hoping they wouldn't hang up in his face, wishing that this time the person on the other end would actually buy his product. The next person on his list was someone named Gina Brown. . . .

Gina contemplated not answering the phone that day. After all, chances were good it would be just another one of those phone salesmen trying to get her to buy something she didn't want or need. But she answered it anyway. On the other end of the line, Ellejandro started his pitch. Gina knew she ought to hang up, but there was something about the salesman's voice that captured her attention.

The two started talking. Before long, they

forgot the sales call and were chatting about more important things—each other! They ended the call, but Ellejandro knew he had to call Gina Brown back again, this time outside of work.

So he did. Gina and Ellejandro quickly became over-the-phone friends, getting to know each other a little better after each conversation. The two decided to meet face-to-face sometime. When they met, they hit it off so well, they started dating regularly. In Ellejandro, Gina found a man who was all she'd prayed for, a man who was a committed Christian and a good person.

"We met each other, and we just clicked and everything was fine," Gina laughs now. "We continued to go out, and the next thing you know, he asked me to marry him! I had been praying that God would bring someone like him into my life."

36

HER NAME
WAS GRACE

"Grace Miller, RN" her name badge said. She was a
nurse, a woman in her midfifties with short, curly
hair who worked at the Boca Raton, Florida,
medical clinic where Jodi Jantomaso went for health
care. Though the two had never really met, Grace
always greeted Jodi with a warm smile and a wave
whenever Jodi came into the office.

But that spring Friday in 1988 Jodi didn't notice
whether or not Grace was on duty. She had another
thing on her mind—her 2:00 P.M. abortion appointment that afternoon. She had arrived at the clinic at
10:00 A.M. for the preliminary blood work and
preparations. Now she sat in the waiting room,
feeling helpless and afraid.

She hadn't intended for things to work out this
way. Twenty-seven years old, Jodi had already
been through a painful divorce and had—until
recently—been very much in love with a man

named Michael. They'd met at the posh resort in Boca Raton where Jodi worked managing the spa and fitness facility. Young, fit, and attractive, she'd quickly caught Michael's eye at the spa. He was handsome as well as wealthy and fun to be around. It wasn't long before they were dating. Soon Jodi moved in with Michael so they could be together more.

"Spiritually, I was at a low point," Jodi admits now. Turning her back on what she knew God wanted, she chose to pursue happiness in the form of her lover, Michael. Together they talked of marriage, children, and living happily ever after.

While Michael was away on a business trip, Jodi found out she was pregnant. She was so excited about telling him the good news! He would return on February 14, 1988, so Jodi planned a special Valentine's surprise to reveal to him that he would be a father.

When he walked in the door on Valentine's Day, he seemed distracted, or tired, or both. Jodi was nearly bursting with excitement. She handed him a gift, a baby's rattle she'd wrapped to clue him in to the pregnancy.

"He opened the rattle, looked at me, and said . . . nothing. I said, 'We're having a baby!' He got up from the table, looked at me, and said, 'Well, things have changed now.'"

And then he dropped the bomb. While on his business trip, he had decided to leave Jodi for another woman—his attorney, Maria. He spoke to Jodi as if the matter were settled. "You'll need to do something about this. Soon."

The next days and weeks were a blur. Jodi found herself sitting in a doctor's office, nervous, numb, and alone, waiting for an abortion. *Oh, God, what am I supposed to do now?* she had cried time and again during the recent days. But God wasn't listening. Or so it seemed.

Before the actual abortion, the doctor wanted to do a preparatory ultrasound. She turned on the equipment and began looking at a fuzzy black image—the inside of Jodi's womb. Suddenly, desperately, Jodi wanted to see what the doctor was seeing. She asked to look at the ultrasound monitor's screen. At first the doctor refused, but when Jodi insisted, the doctor repositioned the screen to allow her a brief glimpse.

Jodi gazed at the near-incomprehensible picture and saw something blinking in the X-ray-like blackness. "What's that?"

"The heartbeat," the doctor replied matter-of-factly.

Jodi was stunned. Tears immediately sprang from her eyes. "I'd been so naive about everything!" she says. "This wasn't just a fetus; it was a live baby!" With that knowledge came a new resolve. Jodi instantly got up from the table, canceled her appointment, got dressed, and went outside, where she sat on the sidewalk, crying.

Oh, God, what am I supposed to do now? she silently sobbed again.

Then Jodi felt someone standing next to her. She looked up and saw the name badge: "Grace Miller, RN."

The kind nurse put a hand on the young

woman's shoulder and spoke. "Jodi, you've made the right choice," she said. "God is going to bless you *and* your baby, and use you more than you could imagine. He'll always provide for you both."

The nurse's words were like a breath of fresh air, and Jodi clung to them, desperate for the hope they offered. Grateful for the encouragement, Jodi thanked the nurse, dried her eyes, and drove home.

Michael was enraged. He tried everything to get Jodi to change her mind, even offering her an envelope containing twenty thousand dollars in cash if Jodi would abort the child. Remembering Grace's words, she refused.

September 29, 1988, Jodi Jantomaso gave birth to a beautiful baby girl, Joelle Aleece. Returning to her Christian roots, Jodi became involved in church again, and when Joelle was only two years old, she joined her mother in singing and performing for their delighted congregation.

Several years after that, Jodi met and fell in love with a Christian musician, Eric Jaqua. They married, and now all three—Jodi, Eric, and Joelle—are involved in speaking and performing for churches and charities nationwide. Inspired by "Grace Miller, RN," they also invest their time in ministering to women who, like Jodi, have found themselves in a crisis pregnancy situation.

The story doesn't end there, though. In 1995, Jodi and Joelle went back to that medical clinic in Boca Raton, hoping to find Grace Miller and thank her in person for helping Jodi to choose life.

But Grace Miller wasn't there. A look at the

payroll records from 1988 revealed that *no* Grace Miller had worked at the clinic. Unbelieving, Jodi asked to speak with her former doctor at the facility. Thankfully, the doctor remembered Jodi and came out to greet her.

Jodi explained the situation. To her surprise, the doctor shook her head and said, "There's never been anyone by the name of Grace who's ever worked here."

Then Jodi realized that God was listening when she cried to him for help so many years before. In response, he'd sent an angel of comfort—one appropriately named Grace—to bring hope and courage to Jodi for a few brief, critical moments. And by doing that, he had saved both a child and a mother at the same time.

"Grace left such an impression on me," Jodi says today. "She touched me by her kindness and words—words from God for me. They're never forgotten."

37

A FATHER'S
PRAYER

John Elefante believes in prayer. The former lead
singer of the group Kansas has seen its power time
and again. The invitation for him to even join
Kansas was an answer to a prayer twenty-five
hundred people had prayed at a massive Bible
study. John was a new Christian then, trying to
decide how his faith would impact his career as a
musician.

Quite frankly, John didn't even pray when he
bought the shoes. He just wanted comfortable,
nice-looking shoes to wear, so he bought a pair of
Doc Martens. He had no idea those shoes would
one day trigger an answer to something he and his
wife, Michelle, were praying about: children.

John and Michelle felt they were ready for
parenthood. "We were trying to have kids and had
a few problems, so we were casually talking about
other options." They were also praying that God

would help them know which direction he wanted them to go in regard to children. The couple was really in no hurry, though, and was satisfied to pray and talk and wait on the Lord for direction.

In 1993 John performed at a Harvest Crusade in California. Backstage after the show, he noticed a woman he did not know walking directly toward him. John paused to talk, assuming she was a fan who might want an autograph or something.

The woman startled John. "You would be the perfect father for a baby to be born in about five weeks!" An earnest discussion ensued about adopting this child.

John and Michelle were nervous going through the whole adoption process. They prayed for God's will to be done, filled out the paperwork, and paid the appropriate preliminary fees. It came time for the birth parents to make a choice. They interviewed John and Michelle and twenty other couples wanting to adopt the child!

Next came the waiting. The Elefantes could do nothing while the birth parents discussed their options. The news came: John and Michelle were chosen as adoptive parents for a beautiful baby girl they called Sammy.

Little did John know that the answer to his prayer was actually triggered by his shopping habits. "When they asked the natural father why he chose us, he said because he liked my shoes. I would have wanted a better answer, but God chooses the foolish things of the world. In the Old Testament, it was a donkey, in the nineties—Doc Martens."

A few years later the Elefantes adopted a little brother for Sammy, naming him Daniel. After experiencing the way God brought these children into his life, John is grateful that God answers prayer. "God wanted these children in our lives and he made it happen. I wouldn't trade them for *anything*. If God came to me right now and said, 'I'll trade you for two biological children,' I'd say, 'Nope. I've got them.'"

38

LATE-NIGHT
TELEVISION

Jim Smith lay awake on the bed, cursing the
darkness and pleading with God to erase it at 1:30
A.M. that warm summer night. It seemed like his
life had been filled with darkness lately, no matter
what time it was.

Jim had been a Christian since high school,
active in church and a leader among his peers.
During those days, Jim and his best friend,
Nicholas, had been inseparable. They had both
vowed to take the world for Christ. But, as often
happens, Jim and Nick grew up and went their
separate ways. Nick married and moved to another
state. Jim married also and settled near where he'd
grown up. The two friends kept in touch, mostly
just trading Christmas cards each year.

As the years rolled on, Jim wavered in his
belief—at times on fire for God, at other times
allowing the cares of this world to overshadow his

commitment to Jesus. That was what had brought him to this point. Several months prior, he'd realized the damage done by ignoring his relationship with Jesus, so he recommitted himself to Christ and pledged to be the man God wanted him to be.

The only problem was that he'd effectively led his family in straying from God, too, and they weren't quite as ready to return as he was. His wife, Candy, an accomplished medical professional, had allowed her career, her friends, and even her husband to distract her from her own commitment to God. Now she was enjoying her unhealthy lifestyle and was unwilling to change.

The friction in Jim and Candy's marriage mounted to the point where the couple even considered divorce. Jim moved to an apartment nearby and spent nights going back and forth from the couple's home to his lonely apartment.

On this night when Jim was visiting the family, he and Candy had a fight. They'd already made plans for him to stay the night, so in frustration Jim went to bed while Candy stayed up a while longer to watch some late-night TV.

It was 1:30 in the morning, and Jim was praying, begging God to heal his marriage and to give him courage to face another day. Broken, he just didn't know what to do. He was exhausted, but sleep wouldn't come. Angry and hurt, Jim felt totally alone.

At 1:45 A.M., Jim looked up to see Candy standing in the doorway, a surprised look on her face. "Nicky is on television—right now!"

Jim bounded out of bed and into the living room. True, there was his old buddy Nick, a guest on the Christian talk show *The 700 Club*. For some reason, the TV station was airing a rerun of the show to fill its early morning programming. Nicky was talking about a book he'd written, an encouragement for families to draw closer to God and each other.

"As soon as I heard Nick's voice," Jim reports now, "the Spirit of God just came over me like a wave. I experienced God's presence in a way I haven't felt him in years. I felt him telling me, 'If you just get through this [current difficulty], you'll see how mightily I'm going to bless you.'"

Jim and Candy's problems didn't disappear the next morning; they are still working through some of their difficulties. With tears in his eyes, Jim says, "Seeing Nicky right at that moment was an answer to prayer. *That* was my miracle."

39

CHANGING
TIMES

By all rights, Terri Blackstock should have been
happy with her career. Writing romance novels
under two pseudonyms, she had established herself
as a favorite—and sold more than 3 million books
in the process.

But something wasn't right, and Terri knew it.
Writing romantic fiction in the mainstream market
required her to include a strong sexual undercurrent
in her books. The mainstream market also welcomed profanity. As a Christian, Terri felt
increasingly uncomfortable about writing that
kind of fiction.

Still, the money was good, and she was gifted at
writing. Perhaps God didn't mind *too* much. . . .

The struggle within her became too great. She
hated the thought that something she wrote might
become a stumbling block for another Christian.
After much prayer and thought, Terri made a

decision. She would never again write anything that didn't glorify God. If that meant the end of her writing career, so be it.

Her decision posed two problems. She was already under contract to write more romance novels for her publisher. "I knew that under my new commitment to God, I could not write the books I had agreed to write. But I had been paid for them and had lived on that money. I didn't have it to pay back!"

Terri immediately made that a matter of prayer. Although she didn't know how to work out the details honorably, she knew that God could find a way. So she prayed, asking the Lord to help her keep the new commitment she'd made to him.

Then mustering her courage, she informed her publisher of the decision to stop writing mainstream romance. She asked if she might be able to buy back the outstanding contracts, thereby releasing her of the obligation to write books she no longer felt comfortable writing. Her publisher begrudgingly acquiesced but did not understand Terri's perspective. The publisher agreed to allow Terri to buy her way out of the contracts.

Then came the real surprise. When the publisher tallied the amount of royalty money still owed to Terri for previous books, it was more than she needed to buy her way out of the contracts! Even after deducting enough to pay for the cancelled contracts, they still owed her money.

Terri gratefully thanked God for his provision, but there was still another problem—a more personal one: Terri's agent. This woman had been

Terri's ardent supporter—and friend—for over a decade. This friend depended on Terri's work to contribute to both their incomes. Though she knew she must, Terri hated the thought of hurting her friend by discontinuing their work relationship.

So she prayed again, fervently asking Jesus for help and guidance on when and how to break the news to her agent. God affirmatively answered that prayer. Terri's agent unexpectedly called one day to say she'd decided to leave the business and that Terri should find a new agent!

Terri reports, "This woman had been an agent for most of her adult life and was completely focused on it. I would never have imagined that she would give it up for anything. God knew better."

Breaking her ties with mainstream romance publishing, Terri set about writing more wholesome fare for Christians. Within a few years she had become a favorite for her Newporte 911 series. The suspenseful Newport 911 series exhibits her new vision. Terri aims to honor God in her writing.

She testifies, "When I go through trials, I often try to remember all the ways that God answered my prayers a few years ago. It reminds me that he is in control, that he's listening, that he loves me."

40

BACK TO
SCHOOL?

"I knew I was going to finish high school, and
I was going to go to college," says Susan Lee. "I
wanted to so badly, but I just didn't see how I was
going to do it. Where was the money going to
come from?"

As a twenty-one-year-old sophomore at
Christian Heritage College in San Diego, Susan
Lee was older than her peers—and older than her
years. When she was fifteen, she had become an
adult, staying in San Diego while the rest of her
family moved to Los Angeles. Over the next three
years she'd worked her way through high school,
earning good grades and money for living
expenses.

Upon graduation, attending a Christian college
seemed financially unfeasible. Susan struggled to
pay her regular bills and winced over college
tuition and books. She took classes at a junior

college and finally dropped out of school altogether.

It was during that time that she felt God prompting her not to give up on college just yet. "I prayed, 'Lord, I need you to make a huge change in my life' because I'd gotten to a point where I was so directionless. I didn't know what was going to happen to my life."

Over the next few weeks, Susan became reacquainted with old friends from her church and made new friends who were attending Christian Heritage College. "All I heard about [from them] was this school!"

She decided to visit the campus. *Just to go in and get information.* Soon it became obvious that she couldn't afford to pay for tuition. Still, she remembered her prayer and decided to apply for admission anyway.

"I made the decision that this was what I was going to do. God had provided for me financially all my life, and I knew he wouldn't stop now. I knew he wasn't going to let me be stranded."

Not long after that decision, Susan got a call from an aunt she had lived with briefly in the past. "Susan, I got some mail for you a couple months ago."

Susan went to pick it up and saw that it was from the state of California. It seems that when she had dropped out of school before, she'd had an application for a state-funded Cal Grant pending. Now, two years later, they wanted to know if she still wanted the money—which was enough to cover more than half of her expenses at Christian Heritage!

From that point on, Susan became a regular visitor at the Financial Aid Office of Christian Heritage College. She was determined to find a way to pay for this school. "I was persistent. They saw me in that office every day. They were all saying, 'Susan's here. Oh, dear.' But they were very good." In the end, they were able to piece together enough financial aid for Susan to return to school.

41

TROUBLE
WITH TICS

It was the early 1990s, and Michael W. Smith and his wife, Debbie, were worried.

Their eight-year-old son, Ryan, who was otherwise healthy and active, had recurring facial tics. The tics had started suddenly when Ryan was seven and had continued into his eighth year. Without warning, his face would start twitching, sometimes becoming so violent that he would actually fall to the floor.

One doctor diagnosed Ryan's problem as Tourette's syndrome. A counselor suggested that emotional problems triggered the tics. Neither of these diagnoses matched with what Michael and Debbie saw in their son from day to day.

The Smiths did not know the cause of Ryan's problem and were unsure how to treat it. Since modern medicine could offer no help, they decided to treat the tics with prayer instead of pills.

Michael and Debbie began praying for Ryan together and individually. They asked the Great Healer to help their son and to heal whatever was causing the tics.

At first they saw no change. Months passed, and Ryan had not improved. Then one day after prayer together, Michael and Debbie felt an overwhelming sense of peace, comfort, and confidence that God had indeed heard their prayers.

Recalling that moment, Michael says, "I remember at one point Deb and I just praying and just getting up and going, 'You know what? He's going to be OK. He's going to be OK. I think God really heard us.'"

Ryan continued having difficulty. His face would twitch and twitch, and no relief seemed to be in sight. But after that prayer, the Smiths were unphased by the continued problem. "It didn't go away immediately," says Michael, "but we just stood our ground [and said], 'Hey, you know what? God's in control. He's going to be OK.' I just never had a doubt."

So they waited. One month. Two months. Ryan still battled the twitching. Three months. Four months. Then suddenly, at five months, Ryan was healed!

During the period when the tics continued, Michael thought, *Oh, maybe he's not OK. . . .* Then he'd say to himself, *Hey! We've committed him to the Lord and we believe God's healed him.*

Michael says, "Before Ryan's ninth birthday, he had a few more tics. And three, four, five months later—boom! Gone! History!"

42

WARTS AND ALL

Sometimes it seemed to Marty Nagy that he and his brother were cursed. No matter what they tried, neither could rid himself of recurring warts. For Marty, the warts appeared primarily on his right hand, and nothing could make them go away for long.

Sometimes Marty tried burning the unsightly growths off, repeatedly removing them with the heat of a flame. He tried freezing them until they came off. Still, it seemed that just as he'd get rid of one, another would crop up somewhere on his hand. He couldn't keep up with them.

Then two warts started growing right under his fingernails. The larger they grew, the more they pressed on Marty's nails, and the more painful they became. About the same time, a new rash of warts began to cover his hand. Before long Marty had nearly twenty warts on his hand—and the two under his fingernails were getting more painful each day.

In desperation, Marty turned to his friend, a Catholic priest, for help. Marty asked his friend if he would pray for God to heal the wart-covered hand. Perhaps God would have pity and at least make the two under his nails go away.

Following biblical instructions, the priest carefully anointed each of Marty's warts with oil. Then he prayed to Jesus, the eternal Healer, asking God to intervene. After the prayer, Marty checked his hand. The warts were still there—oily, but there. He thanked the priest and went home.

The next morning Marty awoke and realized that he no longer felt pain under his nails. Glancing at his right hand, he was disappointed because it was still covered with the curse. Then he looked more closely. The two warts under his fingernails were gone! Marty decided to wait and see what would happen.

Within a week all the warts were gone.

That was more than fifteen years ago. Although his brother has continued to have wart problems for more than thirty years, Marty reports, "I've never had a wart since."

43

SWEET
REUNION

One look at the three sisters on the stage and
you're tempted to think, *These girls have it all.*
Watching them perform as the Christian R&B
group Out of Eden, it is clear why so many fans
have shown up to see the talented women Lisa
Bragg, Andrea Kimmey, and Danielle Kimmey.

What isn't so obvious, however, is that these
sisters grew up for many years without a dad. As
often happens, their parents divorced when the
sisters were young, and the girls lost contact with
their father for more than ten years.

Yet Lisa, Andrea, and Danielle wanted to renew
that relationship—to be a part of their father's life
again—even though they knew he eventually
remarried and had other children. In the silence
of their hearts, each sister prayed that God would
somehow bring Dad back into their lives.

When the sisters reached their teenage years,

their musical talent sparkled. By 1994 they were signed to a recording contract; they performed worldwide while touring with the Christian group dc Talk. It was then God began to answer their silent prayers.

During the tour, Lisa—the oldest sister—discovered that her father was living in California. With the help of her father's new wife and daughter, Lisa orchestrated a surprise Christmas visit to reintroduce herself to her dad.

Of that happy meeting, Lisa says, "He was crying. . . . It was really awesome." Father and daughter hugged and laughed and spent time getting to know each other once more. Lisa knew she had to share this joy with her sisters. Since she was engaged to be married, she invited her dad to attend her wedding the following September in 1996. "He came to my wedding and gave me away. That's when he and Andrea and Danielle were reunited."

Meeting their dad again was a little nerve-racking at first for Andrea and Danielle. "We met again at Lisa's wedding," Andrea says. "At first I was really nervous and was desperately trying to think of something to say!"

Danielle had much the same experience. "It was pretty weird!" she laughs. "My parents divorced when I was like one or two, and we moved away; so I didn't have any memories of my father."

But it didn't take long for that nervousness to fade. "Now we're making memories," says Danielle, "and the feelings I have are ones of joy, security, and love."

Andrea also feels her dad's love. "After ten years I didn't know what he thought I'd be like, and I didn't want to make a bad impression. But now I see that it doesn't matter to him; I realize he loves me for who I am. . . . I'm so glad that he's in my life."

And it turns out the three sisters weren't the only ones praying for a sweet reunion. Lisa reveals, "It's a blessing [for us] because now we talk and everything. He's there for me; we all know he's there for us.

"It's [also] a blessing for him to see what God has done in our lives, and through that be drawn closer to God. He's always prayed for us to be back together. It was like an answer to his prayer."

44

CUTTING
THE LIFELINE

Twenty-nine-year-old Sigmund Brouwer stared at the cover of *National Racquetball.* As an editor for the magazine, he felt that the cover represented his livelihood.

As a bachelor living in Red Deer, Alberta, Canada, Sigmund was able to keep his living expenses low. But the thought of leaving his steady income disquieted him. It was nice to get paid regularly, to buy groceries regularly, and to pay the electric bill regularly.

Still, Sigmund was having that thought again. He was thinking about leaving his career as a magazine editor to pursue what he really wanted to do: write books. And the first book he wanted to write was a mystery for teenagers. He wanted to write a whole series of mysteries for kids. Unfortunately, no publisher had agreed with Sigmund yet. Nobody wanted his books.

Sigmund felt he had to make a decision. He had to choose between a safe career at *National Racquetball* and the risky life of a freelance writer—knowing he was an unproven writer to most publishers. Deep inside, though, he knew the choice had already been made. He had to try to follow his dream; it was now or never. He knew he'd be discontented in his "safe" career at *National Racquetball*.

Summoning his courage, Sigmund resigned from the magazine staff and walked out the door without knowing where he would go from there. He only knew that he wanted to be a writer.

Fortunately, Sigmund didn't have to navigate the world of publishing alone. He turned to his most faithful friend and helper, God. He prayed constantly that first month out, asking God to provide and to lead. Praying for strength and courage to pursue his dream, he asked God to bless his determination to write books that would glorify God.

He wrote letters to publishers, encouraging them to take a chance on this new, young talent in Christian publishing. Two weeks passed without a response.

Sigmund swallowed hard, prayed some more, and kept working. Three weeks passed, then four. Finally, after a month on his own, he got the call he'd been waiting for. Victor Books wanted his youth mystery series!

Victor would publish it under the title The Accidental Detectives. They published ten books in that series—and sold about a quarter of a million copies! Sigmund Brouwer had found his answer to prayer, and it was the start of his writing career.

Since then he's written over two dozen books for youth and adults. Many have reached the best-seller status. He's also started the Young Writer's Institute, an organization dedicated to helping kids age nine to fourteen pursue their own dreams of writing.

Interestingly enough, God used Sigmund's career as a writer to answer another of his prayers—a prayer for a godly wife. When his first adult novel, *Double Helix,* came out, his publisher lined up Christian musician Cindy Morgan to perform a reading from the book with Sigmund at a bookseller's convention. The two hit it off and soon had a budding romance. Less than two years later, they were married and enjoying each other's company.

45

NOT JUST
A FAIRY TALE

Terry Noss is the vice president of production for
Hollywood's Rich Animation Studios. He is the
coproducer of the successful animated feature *The
Swan Princess* and its critically acclaimed sequels.
You can see a caricature of Terry Noss
in *The Swan Princess*.

"Our artists caricatured both coproducers,"
Noss chuckles. "Freeze-frame at the very end
of the movie when [lead character] Derek and
[heroine] Odette have just been married and
they're coming out the door. We're the footmen!
I'm the one with the mustache."

Terry Noss does not keep his Christianity a
secret. People know he is working hard to create
wholesome, family-friendly feature films for mainstream audiences. Terry cannot be quiet about his
whole life being a miracle and an answer to prayer.

He was never an exceptionally healthy child

anyway. A tonsillectomy came when he was seven, appendicitis when he was nine. At age eleven, he began to notice aching in his joints. This aching only got worse.

At first doctors thought it was just growing pains, but the pain became so severe in his knees and ankles that he often felt like collapsing. Terry went in and out of hospitals as he was tested for polio and other illnesses. The doctors were eventually able to diagnose the problem: rheumatic fever.

Having such a critical illness seemed like torture to Terry, just now entering junior high. For the next two years Terry spent most of his life in a hospital bed donated to his family. He was unable to attend school, so private tutors had to come to his home to help him learn what other kids his age were learning in school.

One night when Terry was twelve, his family hosted a Bible study with families from their church. People streamed into the Noss home. Children ran around and played. Laughter was heard throughout the house.

After everyone left, Terry broke down in tears. Seeing and hearing all those healthy children enjoying a normal life pained him. He longed to jump out of his bed and go play with the others, but he couldn't do it. Seeing a glimpse of what he was missing overwhelmed him, and the boy was left sobbing in his parents' arms.

That night Terry pleaded with Jesus, "God, please. Heal me!"

When family friends from the Nosses' church

heard about Terry's despair, they requested that Terry's parents bring him to church for prayer. To be sure, members of the church had already been praying for Terry for more than a year, but this time they felt Terry should come to the church for prayer.

The boy's parents agreed, bringing him the next time they went. Following the biblical instructions, they brought Terry before the elders and the deacons of the church, who placed their hands on him and prayed for his healing.

Terry didn't notice change right away. A few days later Terry noticed the pain in his joints lessening. It was still there, but with a marked difference. Could the healing have begun?

Because rheumatic fever can damage the heart, Terry's doctors scheduled a test to check the boy's condition. But even before the tests, Terry could feel the strength returning to his limbs. The chronic pain he'd felt for two years was ebbing away like water from a storm.

The time came for the tests, and the doctors were surprised. Terry's heart tested normal—no damage at all! A few months later Terry was granted permission to return to school. His disease was inexplicably gone!

It's been thirty years since that healing took place, and Terry gratefully reports no more trouble with rheumatic fever or heart problems. The boy is a now a man, investing anew in the lives of children by creating wholesome family entertainment that even a bedridden junior higher would enjoy.

Asked about it today, Terry points to that prayer at the church altar as the turning point in his illness. "It was at that point that the healing really was triggered."

46

HEY, GOD,
CAN I HITCH A RIDE?

Norm Wakefield sighed as another car whizzed
past him on the open freeway. He adjusted his
backpack and stuck out his thumb for the next car,
hoping to hitch a ride back to Westmont College
in Santa Barbara, California. He tried to smile and
appear friendly to passing drivers—then couldn't
help frowning again as yet another motorist zipped
by without a thought.

It was 1961, and twenty-six-year-old Norm
realized that hitchhiking wasn't working. He'd
been on that road for about forty-five minutes
already, waiting, hoping, and praying for a ride.
As Norm prayed, he got a strong feeling that this
wasn't what God had planned for him this day.

Norm paused and thought about his remarkable
summer thus far. As a student at Westmont, he had
finished the school year with one hundred dollars
still owed on his account. Around that time, he'd

also been offered a summer job as assistant director of a camp for teenagers. The problem was that the camp was located in southwestern Virginia—literally a continent away from his school. The camp couldn't pay much for Norm's work. He'd do well just to break even at summer's end.

Several of his friends advised him to stay in California and earn money to pay his school bill. Still, as Norm prayed about the decision, he sensed God leading him to Virginia to spend his summer ministering to teenagers. So he left California, trusting God to provide the one hundred dollars needed to pay off what he owed.

About six weeks into the summer—unknown to Norm—several of his high schoolers took up a collection to pay off his school fees. God had used them to meet Norm's need. As an extra blessing, another person had donated a one-way bus ticket for Norm to visit his brother in New York when the camp ended.

Norm knew that God could be trusted to meet his needs. Right now, though, what Norm needed most was an all-expense-paid ride back to California—and he wasn't going to get it standing out here on this New York freeway.

Gathering up his bags, Norm prayed quietly as he trudged back to his brother's home in Buffalo. He asked Jesus to lead him and to provide the way for him to get back to school. He also confessed to God that even if he did get back to Westmont, he still didn't have the money to pay the upcoming semester's tuition and fees!

When Norm arrived at his brother's house, he

explained that he had prayed and felt that God had another way for him to return to school. Just then a neighbor interrupted, "There's an ad in the paper for a company that needs a car to be driven out to California. Maybe you should call."

Norm called. The company had a car that needed to be delivered to a place about ninety miles away from Westmont College. Norm volunteered, then gathered his things once more and headed to the car owner's office. Along the way, he prayed about another detail—gas money! Although Norm now had a car that could take him across the continent, he still didn't have any money to fuel the trip.

Norm stood in the office of the company's manager, receiving instructions for his journey— and still wondering to himself what to do about gas money. As they were talking, the manager's phone rang. On the other end were two men who needed a ride to Los Angeles—and who were willing to pay all the expenses for the trip! Norm silently thanked Jesus for his wonderful provision and quickly agreed to take on these new passengers.

A few days later Norm walked onto the campus of Westmont College, happy to have made it back in time to attend his classes. Then he discovered that while God was answering his prayers for transportation on the East Coast, he had also been busy answering his prayers on the West Coast.

Norm reports, "When I got back to school, I was surprised to find that I had a full-tuition scholarship waiting for me that would pay for the remainder of my schooling!"

He smiles when remembering the way God answered those prayers of a student back in 1961. "You'd better believe there was a lot of prayer and thanks for God's care. It was probably the greatest faith-building experience of my life."

47

STRANDED!

It seemed like a perfect beginning for a tragic ending. Two young women, on summer break from college, were stranded along the freeway running through the southern California desert. Only an hour from midnight, Amy Wakefield could almost picture the newspaper headlines: "Coeds Abducted! College Girls Leave for California, Disappear on the Way! Murdered Women Found Only Yards Away from Broken-Down Car!"

Amy shivered involuntarily and turned to her friend and driver. "Exactly where are we, Lori?"

"I'm not sure. I wasn't really paying attention to the signs."

Amy sighed. After spending the school year studying at Arizona College of the Bible in Phoenix, she was headed up to Washington State for a much-needed vacation at Lori's home.

Climbing into Lori's Mustang, the two girls had planned to go from Arizona west to California, then north to Washington.

They sat by the side of the road wondering what they should do next. A few moments ago the car had emitted a loud clunk; the engine had quit, leaving Amy and Lori to coast to the side of the freeway. They were stranded and afraid.

The girls had heard enough horror stories about stranded motorists who were robbed or beaten by criminals who pretended they were stopping to help. Still, what other choice did they have but to try to flag someone down for a ride?

Before they did anything else, the girls decided to pray. Sitting in the vehicle in the middle of the night, they asked their Father in heaven to help and protect them in this crisis. Comforted some by the prayer, they got out of the car, raised the hood to signal distress, then returned to their seats, waving a T-shirt flag out the window to try and capture other drivers' attention.

One car flew past, then another. Semitrailer trucks rumbled by without so much as slowing down. The girls wondered if they'd be stuck out there in the desert all night.

Finally, around 11:30 P.M., the highway grew quiet. Amy and Lori sat in the car, waiting. Suddenly a light shone through the passenger window. Amy stifled a scream. A gruff male voice asked, "What's the problem?"

A man was standing outside the car shining a flashlight inside. Apparently he'd stopped his car up the road a bit and walked back. Since it was night and the hood was up, neither Amy nor Lori had seen him approach.

Amy started to respond to the stranger, then noticed a flicker from the flashlight bounce off the man's glasses. She also realized that she recognized the voice!

"Dave? Dave Mielke? Is that you?"

"Well, yes." Then he looked more closely into the car and suddenly relaxed and smiled. "Amy Wakefield! What are you doing out here at this hour?"

Dave had been one of Amy's instructors at Arizona College of the Bible. He was traveling with his wife to California that night when he saw the broken-down Mustang. Having heard his own horror stories about would-be good Samaritans abused by crooks who posed as distressed motorists, he was reluctant to stop and help— especially at this time of night! But as he drove past the car, he felt a strong compulsion to stop. It was as if God himself was ordering Dave to return and help. So, unsure of the outcome, he pulled off the road and trekked about one hundred yards back to where Amy and Lori waited.

The Bible teacher and his wife drove Amy and Lori to the next town, Indio, California. He helped the girls get the Mustang towed to a garage and made sure they were safe in a motel before he left them.

Amy now says of the experience, "Of all the people who could have stopped on the road that night, God sent an angel named Dave Mielke— someone I trusted and who cared about me—as an answer to my prayer. Isn't that cool?"

48

LOST AND FOUND

The security guard standing in front of the bank's glass-enclosed night depository was both polite and firm. "I'm sorry, ma'am. The night deposit is jammed and not accepting any envelopes."

Zahea (pronounced Zuh-HAY-ya) Nappa received the news with a worried frown. It was 1991, and she had traveled by bus and subway from her work in Virginia to her bank in Washington, D.C., to deposit her paycheck. Having just recently moved to Virginia from D.C., she hadn't gotten around to switching banks yet. Thus, every payday she made this trek to the night depository to replenish her checking account.

But not this Friday. With the depository jammed, how would she deposit her money? The thought of making this trip again tomorrow or Monday wasn't a pleasant one. Plus, wasn't that her bus coming down the street? She didn't want to miss that. . . .

"If you'd like, ma'am," the security guard offered kindly, "I'll take your check inside the bank tomorrow morning when I come to work."

He seemed so trustworthy and customer-friendly that Zahea agreed, handing over her endorsed paycheck and deposit slip with grateful thanks. Then she ran to catch the bus home for a restful weekend.

Saturday morning Zahea began to doubt the wisdom of giving her paycheck to a complete stranger. She called the bank just to make sure the friendly guard had deposited it—and was informed that no deposit had been made. The "guard" had been nothing more than a con man, stealing deposits from unsuspecting customers by passing himself off as an employee of the bank!

Zahea felt sick. She felt so foolish that she didn't even report the robbery, determining to try to scrimp her way to the next payday without her money.

Back at work the next week, a coworker named Chuck noticed Zahea skipping lunch and being particularly frugal—something a bit out of character for her. Out of compassion, Chuck asked, "Zahea, are you short of money for some reason?"

Since he was both a Christian and a friend, Zahea confessed her error over the weekend. Chuck responded by suggesting that they pray, right there and then. They asked God to somehow, someway restore the money that had been lost. Encouraged, they both went back to work.

Zahea made it through the next several days, a bit thinner and a bit wiser for her recent experience. As the weekend approached, she began to make preparations to celebrate the upcoming Easter holiday at her church.

As she left the office to head home, Chuck stopped her at the door. "I have an Easter card for you."

"Thank you, Chuck." Zahea took the envelope and turned once again to leave. Chuck stopped her once more.

"Aren't you going to read your card?" Zahea promptly opened the card to read the sentiment her friend had noted inside.

What she found was the exact amount of money that had been stolen from her! Zahea was stunned and surprised. "Is this a loan?"

Chuck shook his head and grinned, explaining that many people had contributed to the restoration of her lost wages—but he refused to reveal their names. Zahea could only assume it was some of her coworkers who cared enough to share from their own paychecks to make up for hers. God had answered the prayer she and Chuck had prayed just days earlier in that same office building. Zahea thanked God for answering her prayer.

"I have often heard that God protects children and fools. God certainly protected this fool, and he restored my lost wages through the charity of others during the Easter season!"

49

POST-OP
(MIKE'S STORY)

Something was trying to kill me. I could feel it in my gut.

This was supposed to be a simple operation. Though only thirty-three years old, my gallbladder had become so diseased it resembled an old man's and was causing me great pain, making it impossible for me to eat. The surgeon recommended the standard treatment: remove the gallbladder.

I agreed, eager to be rid of the malfunctioning organ. Two days after Christmas in 1996, I entered the hospital for a routine surgery. The anesthesiologist administered the anesthesia, and I was soon ushered into a dark and dreamless sleep.

Ouch! Something was wrong. I couldn't open my eyes or move a muscle, but I could *feel* someone tearing inside my stomach. The pain was unbearable, but I couldn't scream. Had I awakened before the surgery was over? I managed a weak thought. *Help me, Lord. . . .* Moments later I welcomed the darkness that swirled back into my consciousness.

The next time I awoke I knew the surgery was over because I opened my eyes and saw myself in the recovery room. The pain in my stomach, where the surgery had been performed, was overwhelming. I groaned and immediately tried to sit up, not caring that the two nurses near me were trying to hold me down. *This isn't supposed to hurt this much!* I thought. *Something is wrong.*

Apparently I was too strong for my two helpers. The nurse in charge quickly sent the other running to get help to hold me down. I was dangerously close to ripping the IV out of my arm and could possibly tear the fresh stitches in my stomach.

I knew I needed to relax, ignore the pain, and lie back down, but I wasn't strong enough to do it myself. I grabbed on to the metal bar of my bed and became aware of the one nurse left behind still trying to calm me down.

"Pray for me," I croaked to her. Then I demanded it. "Somebody pray for me!"

"OK, OK, Just lie—"

"Pray for me!"

"OK." She took a deep breath and placed her hand on my arm. "Heavenly Father . . ."

As soon as she spoke that name, a sense of peace flooded through me, starting at my head and trickling all the way down to my toes. I felt the Holy Spirit saying, "I'm here. No matter what happens, I'm here."

I watched my hand relax its grip on the bar. I still felt pain, but I was in control of my body once more. Slowly, I lay back onto the gurney. The nurse kept praying. To be honest, I don't know what she said, but I watched her lips move as she continued praying for me.

"Read to me," I said. "From the Bible. Read to me." More medical staff arrived and were beginning to surround me.

"Get me a Bible," the nurse commanded. I saw someone pass a book into her open hand. She flipped it open, paging through to find what she wanted. Then she began to read, "'The Lord is my Shepherd, I shall not want. . . .'"

I closed my eyes. The merciful darkness soon came swirling back into my mind. *Thank you, Lord,* I whispered to myself. Then I slept.

When I woke again later, all was calm. I was sore and weak, but the agonizing pain had been dulled by pain medication. I was in a private room, now. My wife sat next to me, pale faced.

"You had a rough time in there," she said. "I was really afraid for you."

So was I, I thought. *So was I.*

My operation had had complications. While removing my gallbladder, the surgeon had accidentally spilled scores of gallstones inside my body. He had carefully removed each stone, but that added task had apparently triggered unexpected pain for me.

As I write these words, I still feel the effects of that operation, my body never having fully adjusted to the absence of a gallbladder. I am grateful for that nurse—a woman who, at my point of great need, was willing to pray for me—and for my Father, who paused to answer her prayer.

50

MY ONLY PRAYER

My fellow writer, Lee Maynard, has told a story of his own experience with prayer so eloquently, I thought it best for him to relate it to you in his own words:

We are hunkered down at the base of a rock overhang, the summit far above us, watching the rain fall softly. We are tired from climbing and running from the rain.

My eleven-year-old grandson, Tristan, is with me. He knows about Martian landings and cyber-space, and just when you think that's all he is—an interesting child of a technological age—he names the Greek gods and tells how the citizens prayed to them.

"Maybe we should pray for a way out of here," I say, watching the rain grow heavier.

"Does prayer really work?" he asks. "Would it really get us out of here?"

I think carefully about what to say next . . . for I am not a prayerful man.

I have had my share of hurts and pains in the wilderness. The stings of scorpions. The snapping of bones. Dehydration so severe my eyes stung. But I never prayed over any of that. I always thought that if I put myself into those places, it was up to me to get out. God probably wasn't interested.

Prayer, I have always thought, was the thing you saved for last. But every time I got to the last, there was no time for praying. And when it was over, all I could do was wonder that I was still alive.

And so I never prayed. Except once.

It was 1978. In the early hours, when the tops of trees were still lost in darkness, I parked my truck and stepped into New Mexico's Gila Wilderness. My plan was to hike to 20 miles in, then join up with a group of nine Outward Bound School students and their instructors, a "patrol." I was the school director, and I was worried about this patrol: three New England preppies, a college freshman, three high school graduates from Dallas, and two South Chicago street kids who had been sentenced to Outward Bound in lieu of jail.

I looked forward to hiking in the Gila. Even after half a lifetime spent outdoors, I couldn't seem to see it enough. But it was midsummer, and the sun's heat poured down relentlessly. At midday I stopped, drank some water, and for the first time noticed the heat in my boots.

The boots were not new. I had worn them for

some weeks and thought they were ready for the Gila. I was wrong.

I tried everything for relief: stopped and aired my feet, put on extra socks, quickened my pace, slowed my pace, tightened the laces, applied moleskin. Nothing worked.

I reached camp in the middle of the evening meal, took off my boots and socks, and padded around on the soft forest floor. I inspected my feet and counted eleven blisters, near blisters, and hot spots. Still, I told no one about my problem.

We sat and talked for hours. After two weeks in the wilderness, only one student, a New Englander, seemed disenchanted with the course. He had tried to quit but had been talked out of it by the staff.

In the morning, the New Englander was gone. He had left hours before, thrashing back down the trail I'd come in on. We couldn't just let him go into the unforgiving wilderness. Since I was the extra man, I put on the devil boots and went after him.

I soon realized I wasn't just limping anymore—I was walking as though barefoot on hot glass. As I shuffled and stumbled, I tried to keep my mind above my ankles. Again, nothing worked.

A new sound sucked its way into my consciousness, and I realized it was coming from my boots. I sat on a fallen tree, held my feet out in front of me, and looked at the crimson oozing from the eyelets. If I took the boots off, I would never get them on again.

Eventually the trail came out of the brush and straight into the Gila River, flowing down from the high country through shaded canyons. By the time it got to me, this narrow, shallow river was still icy, and I couldn't wait to feel it against my baking feet. But when the water poured into my boots, the burning sensation was replaced with a thousand stabs that seemed to puncture every blister.

My scream cut through the canyon, and I went face forward into the water. Then I got up and staggered across the river.

Since there was no rational solution to my problem, my mind began to create irrational ones. The answer, obviously, was . . . a horse. If I just had a horse, my feet would no longer be a problem, and I could catch the New Englander.

Like King Richard III, I began to implore, "Give me another horse! Have mercy!" What was the next word? Oh yes. "Jesu."

I knew I had only another hundred paces or so in me, and then I would stop, sit, and wait. I'd probably see no one for days.

The sun was low against my back, and my shadow reached far down the stony trail. I would never get to the end of my shadow. And then I stopped.

The right shoulder of my shadow moved, a bulging darkness down on the trail. A huge mass, motionless now, blocked most of the low sun, an elongated head bobbing up in attention to my presence.

It was a horse. A ghost born of pain.

God, I thought, *the mind is an amazing thing.* It was a beautiful ghost, but I would have to make it go away. So I confronted it directly, dragging myself right up to the horse and grabbing its halter.

It was a real horse.

The animal had a halter and a lead rope but no saddle. Something was going on here that I didn't understand, but I was not going to question it. I gathered up the lead rope and struggled onto the horse's back. "A horse, a horse," I mumbled as it calmly carried me down the trail and into the falling darkness. "Jesu."

The horse walked through the night and did not stop until we got to the trail head, where I found the New Englander sitting on the bumper of my truck. I took off the hated boots, bandaged my feet, and hobbled the horse in a patch of grass. The New Englander and I slept nearby.

At first light two wranglers showed up looking for the horse. They said it had never wandered off before and didn't know why it did this time. They said the horse's name was King.

The rain turns to sleet, and I think maybe Tristan and I will have to sleep out the storm on a mountain where there are no horses. He leans against me, and he is smiling.

"Did you really pray?" he asks. "For a horse?"

"Well . . . I was a little out of it. Mumbling. I'm not sure anything I said would qualify as a prayer."

"I think you did pray," he says. "And you got what you prayed for, and it scared you." As usual, he's gotten to the heart of the matter.

The sleet disappears, and a thick mist suffuses

the mountain. But behind the mist is a bright light, glowing first silver, and then gold.

"I did, didn't I?" I admit. "I *did* pray."

We leave the overhang and start down the mountain, the air thick with the nectar of after-storm. It is one of the best days of my life.

Prayer still mystifies me. Maybe I shouldn't save it for last.

I'd be remiss if I ended this book any other way than to allow you an opportunity to add a fifty-first story—*your* prayer story.

Perhaps as you've read through these pages, God's Spirit began speaking to you, calling you, telling you as he told Lee Maynard that prayer is not something to save for a last resort.

Perhaps it's time for you to pray that prayer that God will always answer—the prayer of a sinner asking forgiveness.

The message is simple. All of us—you included—have done wrong. The Bible calls that sin and tells us that the penalty of sin is eternal death. That's the bad news.

The good news is that God sent his Son, Jesus Christ, to pay the penalty of sin. Jesus gave his life, suffering and dying on a cross, to pay that penalty. And then to show that he was more powerful than sin and death, Jesus came back from the dead, resurrected and bringing an offer of eternal life to all who would believe. He offers that life to you.

Listen to how the Bible describes this:

> For all have sinned; all fall short of God's glorious standard. (Romans 3:23)
>
> The wages of sin is death, but the free gift of God is eternal life through Christ Jesus our Lord. (Romans 6:23)
>
> For if you confess with your mouth that Jesus is Lord and believe in your heart that God raised him from the dead, you will be

saved. For it is by believing in your heart that you are made right with God, and it is by confessing with your mouth that you are saved. As the Scriptures tell us, "Anyone who believes in him will not be disappointed." (Romans 10:9-11)

And so now we are back to you. Would you like to experience the salvation that God offers you? If so, it's only a prayer away.

Open your heart to Jesus right now. Pray to him, and ask him to forgive the failings of your past, to erase the penalty of your sin. Ask him to fill you with his Holy Spirit, to make it possible for you to follow him for the rest of your life—and beyond. Why not do it now?

After you have prayed, please contact a church near you, and let someone know about it. Tell the folks there that you have just given your life to Jesus and would like help to learn more about following him.

And if you think of it, let me know about your prayer, too. I'd love to hear from you. You can email me at

Nappaland@aol.com

I look forward to hearing from you soon.

About the Author

Mike Nappa is founder and president of the Christian media organization Nappaland Communications, Inc. He's a best-selling author who has published more than fifteen books and two hundred magazine articles and has been a featured writer in national TV, radio, and print media. He is a contributing editor to *CBA Frontline* magazine and a columnist for *Living with Teenagers, ParentLife,* and *Christian Single* magazines. His work has also appeared in fine Christian publications, such as *CCM, Christian Parenting Today, Clubhouse, Group, HomeLife, New Man, Profile,* and *Release.* A former youth pastor, Mike makes his home in Colorado, where he and his family are active in their church.

Index